JAPAN

ISBN-13: 978-0-8249-6829-8 (softcover)
ISBN-13: 978-0-8249-6828-1 (hardcover)

Published by Williamson Books
An imprint of Ideals Publications
A Guideposts Company
Nashville, Tennessee
www.idealsbooks.com

Text copyright © 2009 by Debbi Michiko Florence
Illustrations copyright © 2009 by Ideals Publications

Printed and bound in China

Library of Congress CIP data on file

Project Editor: Patricia A. Pingry
Book Designer: Jenny Eber Hancock

10 9 8 7 6 5 4 3 2 1

Kaleidoscope Kids® is a registered trademark of Ideals
Publications

Please Note: The information contained in this book is
true, complete, and accurate to the best of our knowl-
edge. All recommendations and suggestions are made
without any guarantees on the part of the author or
Ideals Publications. The author and publisher disclaim
all liability incurred in conjunction with the use of this
information.

PHOTOGRAPHY CREDITS
Photographs on the pages indicated are used by
permission: Cover, 9, Shinto shrine, Kyoto, Honshu,
Japan © Steve Vidler/SuperStock; 12, Mount Fuji,
Honshu, Japan © Steve Vidler/SuperStock; 44,
Japanese bonsai © Prisma/SuperStock; 50, Children's
Peace, Monument, Peace Memorial Park, Hiroshima,
Japan © Kurt Scholz/SuperStock; 88, Japanese Raccoon
Dog © ZSSD/SuperStock; 90, Red-Crowned Crane © age
fotostock/SuperStock; 92, Steller's Sea Eagles © James
Urbach/SuperStock; 94, Japanese Macaque, Kogen
National Park, Japan © age fotostock/SuperStock.

Acknowledgments

Domo arigato to the many people who have provided encouragement, assistance, and information
for this book. I'd like to especially thank the following people: my editor, Pat Pingry, and my agent,
Jennifer DeChiara; for information, Yasuko Fordiani, Gail Hirokane, Toshie Hatami, Shogo Naka-
mura, Mari Uchishiba, Kohei Asada, Junko Mikami, Lance Hatami, Nancy Castaldo, Dylan Hatami,
Karia McIssac, and Nancy Butler; student interviews, Kristin Berry, Keiko Mantani, Naomi
Okamoto and her students at the Shinjo Elementary School, and Yumie Suehiro and her students at
the Suehiro English School; testing activities, Caitlin Schumacher, Ben Bauer, and Lynn Bauer; for
daily encouragement, Cindy Faughnan, Jo Knowles, Joelle McClure, and especially my husband,
Bob, and daughter, Caitlin.

This book is dedicated with love and gratitude to my mom.
—DMF

JAPAN

OVER 40 ACTIVITIES TO EXPERIENCE JAPAN— PAST AND PRESENT

Debbi Michiko Florence

Illustrations by Jim Caputo

williamsonbooks™

Nashville, Tennessee

Come with Me to Japan . . .

Imagine living in a country of 4,000 islands, 500 volcanoes, and more than 2,000 hot springs. A country of sumo wrestlers, samurai, and kimonos.

Even modern Japan, with its high rises and electronics, remains a land of mystery. Its long history is filled with emperors and shoguns, a tradition of eating raw food, and not just one writing system, but three! We have a lot to learn when we take a look at Japan.

What will you find in this book? You'll discover Japan's long history. You'll learn how to write and speak some Japanese words. You'll explore fascinating places like Mount Fuji and crowded Tokyo. You'll learn how to fold origami, how to use chopsticks, and how to make rice balls. You will learn about schools in Japan and what Japanese kids like to do.

The following pages offer a glimpse into this land of mystery. So fasten your seat belt and let's explore Japan!

—DMF

CONTENTS

Japan, Land of Mystery

Japan's unique architecture of Shinto shrines and Buddhist pagodas, its spewing volcanoes and chain of islands, make this country seem like a land of mystery. Around 4,000 islands make up the archipelago of Japan, but most of those islands are small while others are only large rocks. The four largest islands—Hokkaido, Honshu, Shikoku, and Kyushu—are the crowded homes of over 127 million Japanese. Also part of Japan is the Ryukyu archipelago that stretches 650 miles, one island being Okinawa.

Say It!

Hokkaido (hohk-kah-ee-doh)

Honshu (hohn-shoo)

Kyushu (kyoo-shoo)

Ryukyu (ryoo-kyoo)

Shikoku (shee-koh-koo)

A Shinto shrine in Japan

COUNTRY DIVISIONS

J apan is divided into eight divisions: Hokkaido (the northernmost island); Tohoku, Chubu, Kanto, Kinki, Chugoku (all located on the biggest and most populated island of Honshu); Shikoku (the island directly south of Honshu); Kyushu (the southernmost of Japan's major islands); and Ryukyu. Within these divisions are forty-seven smaller divisions, known as *prefectures* or provinces. All prefectures are under the control of the central government in Tokyo, the capital city.

PONDER THIS

The land area of Japan is 378,000 square kilometers, which is slightly smaller than California.

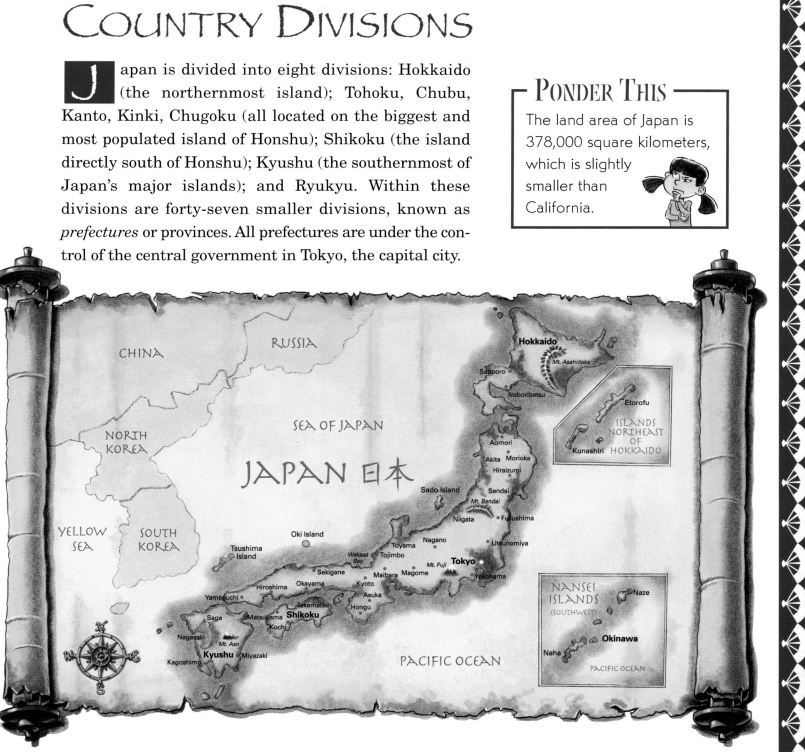

LAND OF THE RISING SUN

Japan's national flag is a red circle centered on a white background. The red circle represents the sun and the white background symbolizes honesty and purity. It is believed that this flag was first presented by a Japanese priest in the late 1200s to Japan's shogun, the country's military leader.

Nihon means "origin of the sun" and is the common word for Japan, whereas *Nippon* is the formal name used on official state documents. The word probably came from China. Because Japan is east of China, from China it looked as though the sun rose out of Japan. Others believed that the sun was born each day and rose out of the Japan Sea. Either way, Japan became the "Land of the Rising Sun."

Say It!

Nihon (nee hohn)

Nippon (ni-pohn)

shinkansen (sheen-kahn-sehn)

PONDER THIS

Look at the flag of the United States. Do you know what the stars and stripes symbolize?

The national flag of Japan

EVERYDAY DIET

From about A.D. 400–700 until 1945, Japan was ruled by emperors who bequeathed the throne to their children. Emperors, and their subjects, believed that the emperor had descended from the sun goddess, a belief that continued well into the twentieth century. Today, however, the emperor and imperial family have only ceremonial and traditional roles.

Today, Japan has a parliamentary form of government with elected representatives who make up the governing body called the *Diet*. The Diet elects the prime minister, who is the real head of the government.

WHAT'S THAT NAME AGAIN?

Tokyo is the capital of Japan and the largest city in the country. The city covers an area of 844.4 square miles (2,187 sq km), but with a population of over 12 million, it is very crowded.

Tokyo, formerly called Edo, was once a small fishing village. In 1868 Edo was renamed Tokyo and declared the capital of Japan. The imperial family still lives on the grounds of the Edo fortress, and while none of the original main buildings survive, the walls, entrance gates, and moats remain.

PONDER THIS

Most of Japan is covered by mountains. How do you think this affects where and how people live?

SO WHAT'S EDO?

Edo was the original name given to the capital city of Japan, now called Tokyo.

FASTER THAN A SPEEDING BULLET

Japan's high-speed trains, known as *shinkansen* or bullet trains, connect major urban areas. A modern transportation system connects the main islands; while the world's longest railroad tunnel, the Seikan Tunnel (33 miles or 53.83 km), links Honshu to Hokkaido.

EARTH'S MYSTERIES

The islands of Japan have different landscapes—from snow-covered mountains to bubbling hot springs, from forests of maple and birch to groves of bamboo. Temperatures range from the cold and snowy winters of Hokkaido to the lush, semi-tropical climate of Okinawa.

SHAKE, RATTLE, AND ROLL

Japan has over 500 volcanoes, 80 of them still active. Some of these volcanoes continually smoke, rumble, and steam. Every now and then one explodes and sends lava down the mountainside. Japan's tallest mountain, Mount Fuji, is a volcano.

The Japanese archipelago sits near the fault formed by two tectonic plates. When these plates shift, earthquakes, typhoons, and tsunamis are caused. When an earthquake occurs under the ocean, it can trigger a tsunami. These giant waves hit the land with such force that they cause massive devastation and flooding.

SO WHAT'S A TSUNAMI?

Tsunami is a Japanese word that means "harbor wave" and is a series of giant waves caused by an earthquake under the sea.

SO WHAT'S A TECTONIC PLATE?

A *tectonic plate* is a large slab of rock in the earth's crust. These plates form a large puzzle and are constantly moving. When the edges of these plates move against each other, they can cause earthquakes, tsunamis, and volcanic eruptions.

NATURAL HOT WATER HEATERS

Japan sits on unstable tectonic plates that produce earth-quakes and hot springs, called *onsen* by the Japanese. These are pools of water that are naturally heated by the hot magma from deep inside the earth. There are over 2,000 volcanic hot springs in Japan. Many are connected to *ryokan*—traditional Japanese guest houses—that are much like bed and break-fasts. Each onsen has a different water temperature and contains different minerals. Some onsen contain sulfur, which makes them smell like rotten eggs! Japanese believe that certain minerals help relieve various ailments like digestion or skin problems.

Say It!

onsen (ohn-sehn)

ryokan (ryoh-kahn)

KEEP THE RULES

Every onsen has strict protocol. A bather first rinses off in a shower, then enters the hot spring to relax and soak. There is no swimming or loud noises, just relaxation and whispered conversation. It is important not to rinse off after getting out of the hot spring, because it takes hours for the minerals to soak into the skin.

SO WHAT'S A TYPHOON?

Typhoon is a Chinese word that means very strong wind. We call these hurricanes in the United States.

ON A CLEAR DAY, YOU CAN SEE FUJI

Mount Fuji, at 12,385 feet (3,776 m), is a volcano that last erupted in 1707. It is also one of the most photographed mountains, as its sides gently slope toward the plain below, and most of the year, its peak is covered with snow. More than 200,000 people climb this spectacular mountain each year, usually during July and August. The Japanese call the mountain *Fujisan*. Mount Fuji is a little over 60 miles southwest of Tokyo, and on a clear day it is visible from the city.

JAPANESE ALPS

Three-fourths of Japan is covered by mountains. Tall mountain ranges, the Japan Alps, run down the center of the Japanese archipelago like a spine. In central Honshu, Japan's main island, the majestic Japan Alps rise with peaks reaching 9,800 feet (3,000 m).

SO WHAT'S AN ARCHIPELAGO?

An *archipelago* is a chain of islands.

Mount Fuji on a clear day

MAKE A
VOLCANO

*Make this volcano outdoors, if you can.
If not, cover the work area with plastic sheeting
and lots and lots of newspapers.*

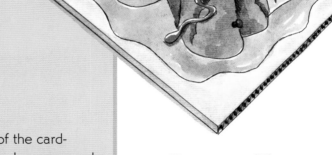

WHAT YOU NEED

- Small plastic juice tumbler
- Cardboard
- Air-dry clay
- 3 tablespoons water
- Red food coloring
- 1 ½ tablespoons baking soda
- 3 tablespoons vinegar

WHAT TO DO

1. Place juice tumbler in the center of the cardboard base. Using the clay, shape a volcano around the cup. Add ridges and slopes to make it look like a real volcano. Do not drop any clay into the cup. Set aside to air-dry according to clay instructions.

2. Pour the water into the top of volcano. Add enough food coloring to turn the water red. Add baking soda to the water. Stir well to dissolve soda.

3. Add vinegar to the soda water and watch the volcano erupt.

Note: The combination of vinegar and baking soda creates carbon-dioxide bubbles that will overflow from the cup.

PONDER THIS

Fuji-san is classified as a stratovolcano, or composite cone, a type of volcano characterized by a gentle lower slope becoming steeper at the top. These volcanoes are some of the most picturesque but most deadly of the volcano types. Other stratovolcanoes include Mount St. Helens in the state of Washington and Mount Etna on the island of Sicily.

Reading and Writing Japanese Style

The Japanese have three writing systems—*kanji*, *hiragana* alphabet, and *katakana* alphabet—and use all three at once! Some Japanese texts are printed in horizontal rows and read from top to bottom, left to right. This is like our English texts and is known as Western style. Other books are printed in traditional Japanese style, with vertical columns that read from top to bottom, right to left. When the Western style is used, books open from right to left. When the traditional Japanese style is printed, books open from left to right.

WRITING SYSTEMS

Kanji are complicated characters adopted from the Chinese. Each character stands for a whole word or an idea. It would be as if a circle stood for the word ball, and whenever we saw a circle we would automatically say "ball." Or we could also write out in our regular alphabet b-a-l-l and we would also read that as "ball." Some Japanese words and ideas have no corresponding kanji, however, so they must be written in alphabet form. The two alphabets, hiragana and katakana, consist of individual letters. These are used for grammatical endings and for the spelling out of words.

Kanji

The Japanese did not have a written language until the Asuka period of the sixth or seventh centuries (A.D. 552–645), when they imported the Chinese character style of writing. This writing is known as *kanji,* which uses ideograms. Ideograms give no indication of the pronunciation, so the Japanese pronounce the Chinese characters very differently than do the Chinese.

In kanji, characters can be combined to make a new word. For instance, the character for "person" combined with the character for "shape" creates the ideogram for "doll." There are tens of thousands of kanji, and in order to read them, they must be memorized. By high school, students are expected to know over 1,500 kanji; a person needs to know about 3,000 kanji to read a newspaper.

Kanji are used for writing nouns, adjectives, adverbs, and verbs. Grammatical endings, however, cannot be written in kanji.

Say It!

Hiragana (hee-rah-gah-nah)

Kanji (kahn-jee)

Katakana (kah-tah-kah-nah)

⌐So What's an Ideogram?

An *ideogram* is a written character that stands for a concept or thing but with no indication of its pronunciation.

TWO MORE WAYS OF WRITING

In addition to kanji, there are hiragana and katakana scripts. These writing styles are not based on ideograms but upon 46 syllables, five of which are vowels: *a, i, u, e, o*. The remaining 41 characters are syllables with one vowel combined with a consonant. The alphabets—hiragana and katakana—were created when the Japanese adapted and simplified Chinese characters during the Heian period (794–1185).

KATAKANA

Katakana is for sounds, foreign, or "loan," words, and foreign names and geographical places which cannot be written in kanji. Examples of katakana words are *wan wan* which means "woof woof," and *aisu kurimu* which means "ice cream."

HIRAGANA

Hiragana is the writing that Japanese use to write original Japanese words and is the first writing system taught to Japanese children. That is why most books for young children are written in hiragana. Examples of hiragana words include *inu,* which means "dog," and *neko,* which means "cat."

LET'S WRITE JAPANESE!

WHAT YOU NEED

- Copy of *hiragana* alphabet
- Pen or pencil
- Paper

WHAT TO DO

Following the alphabet and pronunciation for *hiragana*, find the Japanese characters and write these words in Japanese.

English	Japanese	characters
ant	*ari*	(a-ri)
cat	*neko*	(ne-ko)
eye	*me*	(me)
chair	*isu*	(i-su)
door	*to*	(to)
bird	*tori*	(to-ri)

Let's practice

Hiragana Alphabet

ん	わ	ら	や	ま	は	な	た	さ	か	あ
un	wa	ra	ya	ma	ha	na	ta	sa	ka	a
		り		み	ひ	に	ち	し	き	い
		ri		mi	hi	ni	chi	shi	ki	i
		る	ゆ	む	ふ	ぬ	つ	す	く	う
		ru	yu	mu	fu	nu	tsu	su	ku	u
		れ		め	へ	ね	て	せ	け	え
		re		me	he	ne	te	se	ke	e
	を	ろ	よ	も	ほ	の	と	そ	こ	お
	wo	ro	yo	mo	ho	no	to	so	ko	o

Katakana Alphabet

ン	ワ	ラ	ヤ	マ	ハ	ナ	タ	サ	カ	ア
un	wa	ra	ya	ma	ha	na	ta	sa	ka	a
	リ			ミ	ヒ	ニ	チ	シ	キ	イ
	ri			mi	hi	ni	chi	shi	ki	i
	ル	ユ	ム	フ	ヌ	ツ	ス	ク	ウ
	ru	yu	mu	fu	nu	tsu	su	ku	u
	レ		メ	ヘ	ネ	テ	セ	ケ	エ
	re		me	he	ne	te	se	ke	e
ヲ	ロ	ヨ	モ	ホ	ノ	ト	ソ	コ	オ
wo	ro	yo	mo	ho	no	to	so	ko	o

Let's practice

LET'S SPEAK JAPANESE

Japan's writing system is complicated, but sounding out the words is simple if you break them into syllables. All syllables receive the same amount of stress or emphasis, so you won't see any accented syllables. Vowels always have the same sound in every word.

Vowel Sounds:
a (ah) as in car
e (eh) as in pet
i (ee) as in pink
o (oh) as in toe
u (oo) as in flu

LET'S COUNT TO 10

NUMBER	JAPANESE	SOUNDS LIKE
1	*ichi*	(ee-chee)
2	*ni*	(nee)
3	*san*	(sahn)
4	*shi*	(shee)
5	*go*	(goh)
6	*roku*	(roh-koo)
7	*shichi*	(shee-chee)
8	*hachi*	(hah-chee)
9	*kyu*	(kyoo)
10	*ju*	(joo)

Try It!

Try writing out the list of words in "Let's Write Japanese" on page 17, but this time, use the *Katakana* alphabet.

COMMON PHRASES AND WORDS

ENGLISH	JAPANESE	SOUNDS LIKE
Hello!	*Konnichiwa!*	(kohn-nee-chee-wah)
Good-bye.	*Sayonara!*	(sah-yoh-nah-rah)
Good morning.	*Ohayo gozai masu.*	(oh-hah-yoh goh-zah-ee mah-su)
Good night.	*Oyasumi nasai.*	(oh-yah-su-mee nah-sah-ee)
How are you?	*Ogenki desu ka?*	(oh-ghen-kee deh-su kah)
I am fine.	*Genki desu.*	(ghen-kee deh-su)
Thank you!	*Arigato!*	(ah-ree-gah-toh)
Yes	*Hai*	(high)
No	*Iie*	(ee-ee-eh)

Mysterious Traditions

Japan is an ancient country with firmly established traditions and customs. It has rules and traditions for every day and every occasion. These include the customs of bowing and removing one's shoes when coming indoors. Traditional Japanese costumes and home furnishings, traditional religions, and even traditional martial arts are known the world over. Let's take a look at some of these uniquely Japanese traditions.

EVERYDAY TRADITIONS

Instead of shaking hands, Japanese greet one another by bowing. All Japanese, including children, bow when saying "hello," "goodbye," "thank you," "you're welcome," and "excuse me." Men bow with their hands at their sides, while women bow with their hands together. How deep a person bows depends on the status and age of the person. A young person would bow much deeper than would an older person. In casual situations, sometimes a nod will do.

COUNTRY TRADITIONS

In the countryside, called the *inaka*, life moves at a slower pace than in the cities and follows the changing seasons. In the country are large fields of fruit orchards and rice farms. Japanese grow rice on flat plains and on the steep mountains which are terraced. In spring, the rice fields are flooded and small rice seedlings are planted. In autumn, rice is harvested, grapes are picked, and persimmons are laid out to dry.

Say It!

inaka (ee-nah-kah)

DON'T BE RUDE

In Japan, riding on the subway or train usually means riding in silence. Commuters read or text-message but never talk on the phone or talk loudly to their companions. Staring is considered rude, and commuters keep their eyes down or closed.

A REVERSAL OF NAMES

In Japan, a person's last, or family, name comes first. In Japan my name would be Florence Debbi. Only close friends and family use first names, and titles—*san* for adults—are still used. Florence Debbi would be Florence-san to acquaintances, or Debbi-san to friends and family. Even children have titles. An informal title for girls is *chan*. If I were a little girl, my friends and family would call me Debbi-chan. For a boy, the title is *kun*. A little boy named Peter would be Peter-kun.

HOME, SWEET HOME

Although apartments and homes in Japan's big cities have lots of Western touches, Japanese homes in both the city and in the country share some unique characteristics. Because the Japanese never wear shoes inside their homes, the entry will have a place to store shoes. Adults wear slippers inside the house; kids might wear slippers but usually run around barefoot or in socks. If walking on delicate *tatami* floors, however, no one wears even slippers—just socks.

Say It!

futon (foo-tohn)

kotatsu (ko-tah-tsoo)

ofuro (oh-foo-roh)

shoji (shoh-jee)

tatami (tah-tah-mee)

OFURO

The *ofuro* is the bathing area and is not like our bathrooms. The ofuro has a tile floor, a drain, and a very deep tub which is filled with hot water then covered until needed. A person rinses off outside the tub, either with a shower or by scooping water out of the tub and splashing oneself. (This is why there is a drain in the floor.) While sitting on a low stool, a person scrubs his or her body with soap and then rinses well. Now clean and rinsed of soap, he or she climbs into the tub to soak and relax in the warm water.

TATAMI

In Japan today, even modern apartments usually have at least one room with a *tatami* floor, as a reminder of Japanese culture. Tatami is made of straw woven into rectangular mats. Each mat is roughly 35½ by 70 inches (90 cm x 180 cm), although they can also be made in half sizes of 35½ x 35½ inches (90 cm by 90 cm). Since the size of the tatami is standard, tatami rooms must be built with the mat sizes in mind.

FUTON

Futons can be found in the United States, but these futons have wooden frames and double as couches. In Japan, a futon is the bed and consists of a foam mattress and soft quilts, all of which are folded up and put away in a closet during the day. Beds like you sleep on can also be found in Japanese homes.

SHOJI

The *shoji* is a wooden screen with rice-paper panels and functions as a sliding wall. Because Japanese rooms were traditionally small, the shoji screen was designed to slide open to make the living space bigger or to be closed for privacy.

KOTATSU

Traditional Japanese tables are low to the ground and diners sit on pillows on the floor. The *kotatsu* is a low table that has a heater underneath the tabletop. Before the age of central heating, this heater provided extra warmth during cold days.

Just Don't Have a Thing to Wear!

Throughout the world, the *kimono* is recognizable as the traditional dress of the Japanese. Literally translated, *kimono* means "thing to wear," but we know it as the elaborate and beautiful, robe-like silk clothing worn in Japan. Both men and women wear kimonos, but women wear brightly colored ones decorated with elaborate designs. Less formal versions of the kimono include the *happi* coat, which is a short kimono worn as a jacket. The traditional happi coat had a family crest embroidered on the back.

Say It!

kimono (kee-moh-noh)

yukata (yoo-kah-tah)

happi (hahp-pee)

tabi (tah-bee)

geta (gheh-tah)

juban (joo-bahn)

obi (oh-bee)

MAKE A HAPPI COAT

WHAT YOU NEED

- Paper and pen or pencil
- Adult button shirt
- Fabric markers
- Old towel that can be cut up
- Scissors to cut towel
- Stapler with staples

WHAT TO DO

1. Sketch a design for the back of your *happi* coat. This could be a drawing of your favorite animal, a flower, a heart, a shooting star, the sun, or the moon and stars.

2. Draw the design on the back of your shirt with your fabric markers.

3. To make the sash, cut the towel into 2-inch strips the length of the towel. Staple the strips together until you have the length you need to wrap around your waist and tie.

4. Put on your *happi* coat and tie the belt.

The Ritual of Donning the Kimono

Tabi

The first item in the kimono dress is the *tabi*, which are special socks with the big toe separated from the rest of the toes, sort of like the thumb in mittens. This is necessary in order to wear the *geta*.

Juban

Next, a person puts on the *juban*—an undergarment with a white collar that will be visible above the main kimono garment.

Kimono

After the juban, the kimono is put on. The kimono is not fitted to the wearer but is a standard pattern and size. Men and women both wrap the left side of the kimono over the right side.

Obi

The *obi* is the sash tied around the kimono. The obi can be up to thirteen feet long and the bow that is tied in back can be very elaborate. Another person is necessary for tying the obi.

Geta

The last thing the person dons are the geta. These are shoes with thongs that slide between the big toe and the second toe, much like our flip-flops.

PHILOSOPHY AND RELIGION

The two major religions in Japan are Shinto and Buddhism. Other religions do exist in Japan, but the majority of Japanese consider themselves Shintoists, Buddhists, or both. In fact, many national traditions and holidays have their origin in Shinto or Buddhism.

BUDDHISM

Buddhism came to Japan by way of China during the Asuka period (A.D. 552–645) and is based on the idea that all life is suffering. Buddhism focuses on personal spiritual development and teaches the idea that reincarnation will take place until one has achieved enlightenment.

So What Do Buddhists Believe?

- All living things are equal.
- After death, people come back (are reincarnated) to live again.
- When all suffering is gone, *nirvana* is reached and there is no more reincarnation.

So What Do Shintoists Believe?

- People are good; evil is caused by evil spirits.
- Spirits, called *kami*, are in nature and can bring good luck.
- Shinto has no founder and no writings, but many gods.

Say It!

ema (eh-mah)

kami (kah-mee)

omamori (o-mah-moh-ree)

Shinto (sheen-toh)

SHINTO: THE WAY OF THE GODS

Shinto means "the way of the gods" and began around the sixth or seventh century. Shinto is centered in nature and around a reverence for *kami*, gods that inhabit natural things. There are many kami which are worshiped at various shrines throughout the country.

SHINTO ETIQUETTE

When worshipers enter a Shinto shrine, they wash their hands in a basin at the entrance, then clap their hands to frighten away evil spirits. The visitors bow and place food or money on the altar as a gift to the kami. Worshipers write their prayers on wooden plaques, called *ema*, and hang them on trees. Worshipers can also purchase good luck charms, called *omamori*.

THE SHINTO CAT

The story is told of a lord traveling home in a rainstorm who took shelter under a tree in front of a temple. Through the rain, the lord spotted a cat in front of the temple beckoning him to come inside. As the lord ran to the temple door, lightning struck the tree. The lord believed the cat saved his life and, in gratitude, gave much of his fortune to the temple. The cat became a protective kami and statues of a waving cat can be seen in many Japanese restaurants, even those in the U.S.

PONDER THIS

Shinto focuses on purity and cleanliness. When it comes to weddings, Japanese use Shinto traditions. When it comes to funerals, however, they use Buddhist traditions.

JAPANESE SPORTS

L ike kids—and big kids—everywhere, the Japanese love sports. Some sports in Japan are unique to the country, such as sumo and some martial arts. Japanese martial arts were originally developed by the samurai as the arts of war. Martial arts like judo have degrees of achievement signified by the color of the belt. Although sumo is Japan's national sport, it is not the most popular. That distinction belongs to baseball.

LEARN MORE·LEARN MORE·LEARN MORE·LEARN MORE·LEARN MORE·LEARN MORE·LEARN MORE·LEARN MORE

To learn more about Japanese baseball, their teams, and baseball statistics, visit Japan's baseball web site: www.japanball.com

SUMO

Sumo has been around for 2,000 years and can trace its history to Shinto harvest rites and religious traditions. Before a match, the wrestlers lift their legs high and stomp their feet to scare away evil spirits. They throw salt into the ring to purify it. Then the two sumo wrestlers stamp, clap, and raise both hands to show they are not armed before they crouch down and try to push the other down or out of the circle. The wrestler who touches the floor with any part of the body other than the bottom of his foot or who is pushed out of the circle loses the match. The matches usually last about ten seconds.

Sumos oil their hair and pull it into a topknot. They live together in stables where they train and eat a strict diet. Since there are no weight restrictions, the wrestlers are very, very large.

KENDO

Kendo was developed by the samurai and was originally a type of fencing with swords. Today, kendo participants use bamboo swords and wear padded suits.

Say It!

karate (kah-rah-teh)

sumo (soo-moh)

jujutsu (joo-joo-tsoo)

kendo (kehn-doh)

KARATE

Karate began in Okinawa and literally means "empty hand." Karate fighters use kicks, punches, and blocking moves to subdue their opponents and defend themselves with hands, elbows, and feet. This martial art is related to Chinese *kung-fu* and Korean *tae kwon do*.

JUDO

Judo began in feudal Japan as *jujutsu*, and today's judo is a refinement of this original martial art. In judo the fighter uses throwing and grappling techniques to subdue his or her opponent.

PONDER THIS

Ichiro Sasaki of the Seattle Mariners, Daisuke Matsuzaka of the Boston Red Sox, and Hideki Matsui of the New York Yankees are baseball players from Japan.

A NEW ALL-JAPANESE TRADITION

Baseball was introduced to Japan from the United States during the Meiji period (1868–1912). The Japanese love this all-American sport and have made it their own. Today there are two major leagues in Japan: the Central League and the Pacific League. They have team names like the Yakult Swallows, Yokohama Bay Stars, and Seibu Lions.

Holidays and Festivals

Japan has fifteen national holidays as well as numerous local festivals. Even though some Japanese celebrate Christmas, it is not a national holiday; most Japanese celebrations center around Shinto traditions. For almost all celebrations, including New Year's Day and birthdays, the Japanese say *"omedeto,"* which means "congratulations."

Say It!

daruma (dah-roo-mah)

omedeto (oh-meh-deh-toh)

oshogatsu (oh-shoh-gah-tsoo)

NEW YEAR

The most important holiday in Japan is New Year, or *oshogatsu,* which is celebrated for three days—from January 1 to January 3. Businesses close and families spend time together. Beginning in late December, Japanese families prepare for the holiday by cleaning their houses, repaying debts, forgiving arguments, and returning anything borrowed.

GOOD-LUCK CHARM

The *daruma* is a good-luck charm that is a traditional New Year's gift. A daruma looks like a doll's head with white eyes but no pupils. When a person receives a daruma, he or she makes a wish and colors in one eye. The other eye can be colored in if and when the wish comes true.

MAKE A
DARUMA

Fig. 1

WHAT YOU NEED

- Round balloon
- ½ cup flour
- 1 cup water
- Newspaper torn into
    1- to 2-inch-wide strips
- Paintbrush
- Red, white, and black
    craft paint
- Medium mixing bowl

WHAT TO DO

1. Blow up the balloon and tie it closed.

2. In the bowl, combine ½ cup flour with 1 cup water. Stir to make a thin paste. Dip newspaper strips into the mixture, one at a time. Use your fingers to remove excess liquid. Lay overlapping strips in a crisscross pattern over the balloon until it is completely covered. Smooth out the wrinkles. (See figure 1.) Let the balloon dry overnight.

3. After the paper has dried, stick a pin into the balloon and pop it.

4. The knot end is the top of the daruma. Gently press on the opposite end to make a flat surface so the daruma will stand up on its own.

5. Paint the daruma's body red. (See figure 2.) Mix red and white paint to make pink for the face. Paint the eyebrows black and the mouth red. Paint white circles for the eyes, but do not paint the pupils. Set aside to dry.

6. Make a wish, then color the pupil of one eye. When your wish comes true, color the pupil of the other eye.

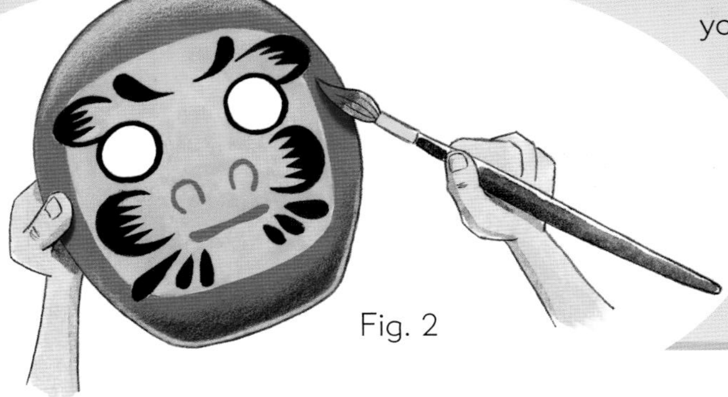

Fig. 2

FOR SOME CHILDREN

November 15 is *Shichi-Go-San,* a day for children. *Shichi* means "seven," *go* means "five," and *san* means "three," which are the ages of the children honored on this day. Children dress in their best kimono and are taken to the local Shinto shrine. The children clap their hands and ring a bell to get the attention of the god (kami) to whom they pray for long life and good health. After the prayers, the children are given *chitose ame*—red and white candies—that symbolize long life.

CLAP CLAP

FOR ALL CHILDREN

Every May 5 is the national holiday for children—k*odomo no hi.* Families display one carp banner, called *koinobori,* for each son in the family. Because the carp has to swim upstream to lay its eggs, it symbolizes strength and determination.

DOLL FESTIVAL

Hina matsuri is a doll festival celebrated every March 3 to honor daughters. On this day, mothers hand down a special set of dolls to their daughters. These dolls are displayed on a tiered stand covered with red cloth. At the top are the emperor and empress, then the ladies-in-waiting and musicians, and, last, the servants. The girl's family prepares special *mochi* (sticky rice cake)—called *hishi mochi*—for the occasion.

Say It!

hina matsuri (hee-nah maht-su-ree)

hishi mochi (hee-shee moh-kee)

kodomo no hi (koh-doh-moh noh hee)

koinobori (koh-ee-noh-boh-ree)

shichi go san (shee-chee goh sahn)

CARP BANNER

Fig. 1

WHAT YOU NEED

- 1 large sheet of colored tissue
- Pencil
- Scissors
- Newspapers
- Colored markers
- Pipe cleaners
- Tape
- Glue stick
- String or piece of yarn

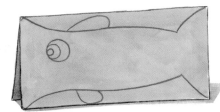

Fig. 2

WHAT TO DO

1. Fold tissue paper in half lengthwise. Draw the shape of a carp or fish the length of the tissue paper and with its top at the folded edge. Draw an open mouth as large as the entire width of the paper. (See figure 1.)

2. Cut out the carp, if you wish, but do not cut along the fold.

3. Cover your work surface with newspapers. Unfold your carp on the newspapers and color it with markers. Cut strips into the fish's tail. (See figure 2.)

Fig. 3

4. Form a circle with the pipe cleaners and tape it to the inside of the carp's mouth. Cut the pipe cleaner if you need a smaller circle or tape two together if you need a larger one. (See figure 3.)

5. Glue the bottom edges of the carp together, leaving the tail and mouth open.

6. Tie a piece of string to the mouth of the carp and hang. (See figure 4.)

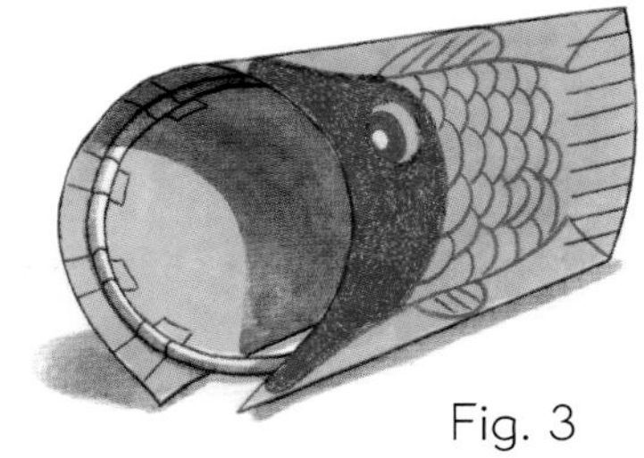

Fig. 4

FESTIVAL FOR ANCESTORS

Obon is a Buddhist celebration honoring deceased ancestors; their families set out lanterns to light the way for these spirits. The obon festival is celebrated with food and a special evening event called *bon odori* that features *taiko* drummers, singing, and dancing.

A BIG DRUM

Taiko is a large Japanese drum struck with two sticks; drummers perform synchronized routines. Taiko was originally used to communicate news, intimidate enemies, and scare away evil spirits. Today, the taiko is a musical instrument used during Japanese *masturi* (festivals).

Say It!

obon (oh-bohn)

sakura (sah-koo-rah)

taiko (tah-ee-koh)

masturi (mahs-too-ree)

LEARN MORE · LEARN MORE · LEARN MORE · LEARN MORE · LEARN MORE · LEARN MORE · LEARN MORE · LEARN MORE

In the United States, people have formed *taiko* groups. Some groups travel and give performances. The San Jose Taiko Group in California is one such group. Check out their kid's web site to learn more! You can watch a fabulous video clip of a taiko performance.
http://209.35.123.104/kidsweb/index.html

Try It!

If you live near a city with a Japan Town, chances are they will have *obon* during the summer. Attend a festival to experience Japanese food and festivities. Visitors are welcome to join in on the dancing.

CHERRY BLOSSOM FESTIVAL

Cherry-blossom viewing has been a Japanese tradition since the seventh century. Japanese cherry trees do not bear fruit; they bloom with delicate pink and white blossoms, called *sakura*, which is the national flower of Japan. Each spring Japanese cherry trees bloom for only a few days before the fragile blossoms fall and are blown away. This temporary beauty reminds the Japanese of the brevity of life and invokes appreciation for the present. While the trees are in bloom, families gather in parks to admire the beauty and delicacy of the Japanese cherry blossoms.

PONDER THIS

In 1912, Japan gave 3,020 cherry trees to the United States as a gesture of friendship. These trees were planted in Washington, D.C., along the Tidal Basin and around the White House. In 1965, Japan gave another 3,000 trees, which were planted around the Washington Monument. Each spring, the capital hosts a Cherry Blossom Festival with a parade and Japanese food, crafts, and music.

LEARN MORE·LEARN MORE·LEARN MORE·LEARN MORE·LEARN MORE·LEARN MORE·LEARN MORE·LEARN MORE

To learn more about the Washington, D.C., Cherry Blossom Festival, visit the National Park Service web site: http://www.nps.gov/nama/planyourvisit/national-cherry-blossom-page.htm

Kids Will Be Kids

What would life be like if you lived in Japan? What would your house look like? Would school be the same as yours? You might be surprised to discover that some things would be similar to your life, and you might be surprised to find out what things might be different. Let's take a look at some aspects of Japanese kids' daily lives.

Say It!

gakko (gahk-koh)

juku (joo-koo)

sensei (sehn-seh-ee)

GOING TO SCHOOL

Education and getting into the best school are very important in Japan. All children, beginning at age six, must attend school, called *gakko*. They attend school for nine years, with six years of primary school and three years of junior high school. Three years of senior high school is legally optional, but most children attend high school.

CRAM SCHOOL

Many students go to school after their regular school, called *juku* or cram school. They study the same subjects as in regular school but have additional help. Students usually begin juku in the fifth or sixth grade to keep up with, or get ahead of, their regular school studies.

Teach to the Tests, Please!

In Japan, children are placed in schools by their test scores. Students must attend the elementary school attached to the high school of their choice, but they must pass a test to get into the elementary school. They can remain at that school until they graduate high school. If a child does not pass the elementary school test, he or she attends the neighborhood school. The child can test again to try and get into a better junior high or high school. After high school graduation, students must pass a test to get into a good college. This test is very important because it will determine the future career of the student.

School Traditions

Japanese students attend school all year, with about fifty vacation days. Every morning the students bow to their teacher (*sensei*), and say, "*Ohayo gozai masu,*" which means "Good morning." In addition, each day the children clean their schoolrooms and the halls. Children spend most of their time studying, taking tests, and doing homework. Students have about three to four hours of homework a day; and during school vacations, students in the fifth grade and higher spend most of their free time studying.

IT'S A SMALL WORLD, AFTER ALL

Do you wonder what Japanese kids your age like to do and eat? Do you think they are similar to you and your friends? Here is how 29 students, ages 7–12, from Yanai-City, Yamaguchi Prefecture, Japan, answered some questions about what they like to do. Write down your answers on the lines provided. How different are your answers from those of the Japanese kids?

What is your favorite subject in school?

"Mathematics," Sayaka, age 7.

"Science and social studies," Sadanori, age 7.

"Physical education," Haruki, age 9.

"Japanese, home economics, physical education," Kazuya, age 11.

"General Matters," Eri, age 11. (General Matters can include things like learning how to cultivate rice, the English language, and researching the local area.)

My favorite school subject is _____

What do you like to do in your free time?

"Play with my friends," Sadahide, age 9.

"Play Nintendo DS," Aika, age 7.

"Read math books," Yuta, age 10.

"Sleep," Hideaki, age 11.

"Play the recorder," Tomoka, age 8.

In my free time, I like to _____

What is your favorite food?

"Peaches," Erika, age 9.

"Fried chicken," Sayaka, age 12.

"Curry and rice," Monami, age 8.

"Strawberries," Kohki, age 8.

"Sushi," Yui, age 10.

"Fermented soybeans," Akihumi, age 9.

My favorite food is _____

What is your favorite game or sport?

"Riding a unicycle," Kaho, age 10.

"Swimming," Miku, age 10.

"Table tennis," Mayu, age 11.

"Dodgeball," Wataru, age 8.

"Baseball," Yusuke, age, 10.

"Soft volleyball," Yuna, age 9.

My favorite sport is _____

What do you want to be when you grow up?

"Carpenter," Yuichi, age 9.

"Pharmacist," Takuya, age 11.

"Preschool teacher," Hikaru, age 9.

"Cartoonist," Rina, age 9.

"Baseball player," Yoshiki, age 7.

"Librarian," Shiori, age 10.

"TV announcer," Asami, age 10.

When I grow up, I want to be _____

PLAY
HANETSUKI

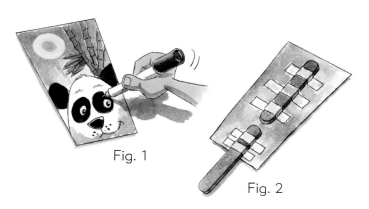

Fig. 1

Fig. 2

WHAT YOU NEED

- 2 *hagoita* and 1 *hane* (see directions)
- 2 people

WHAT TO DO

1. Each player chooses a *hagoita* and stands 2 or 3 feet from the other.

2. One player tosses the *hane* to the other player.

3. The player uses the *hagoita* to hit the *hane* back and forth with an underhand motion.

4. When a player misses, the other player gets a point.

5. The first person to get 5 points wins.

MAKE A
HAGOITA

WHAT YOU NEED

- Pencil
- 2 large, sturdy paper plates
- Scissors
- Colorful markers
- Tape
- 4 large craft sticks

WHAT TO DO

1. Sketch out a large rectangular paddle shape (the diameter of the entire plate) on both paper plates and cut them out.

2. On the front of each paddle, create a colorful design with markers. (See figure 1.)

3. Tape a craft stick to the back of each paddle to give it some strength. Tape a second craft stick to each paddle to create a handle. (See figure 2.)

MAKE A HANE

WHAT YOU NEED

- 1 tablespoon birdseed
- Plastic sandwich bag
- Rubber band
- Scissors
- Colorful tissue paper
- Tape
- Narrow ribbon

WHAT TO DO

1. Place birdseed into a corner of the plastic bag and seal it right above the seeds with the rubber band. (See figure 1.)

2. Cut off the bag about 1 inch above the rubber band. (See figure 2.)

3. Cut out a small square of tissue paper. (See figure 3.)

4. Wrap the tissue around the seed bag so that the ends gather at the top, making a "birdie" or shuttlecock shape. (See figure 4.)

5. Cut feather shapes out of the tissue paper and tape them to the top of the bag. (See figure 5.)

6. Use ribbon to tie around the tissue paper. (See figure 6.)

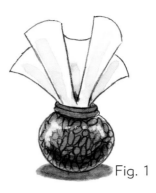

Fig. 1

Fig. 2

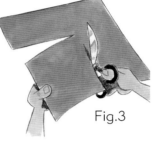

Fig.3

Fig. 4

Fig. 5

Fig. 6

Say It!

hagoita (hah-goh-ee-tah)

hane (hah-neh)

hanetsuki (hah-neh-tsoo-kee)

The Mystery of Serenity

Serenity and peace are very important to the Japanese. There are various traditions that impart this sense of peace, including tea ceremonies, *bonsai*, *ikebana*, and Japanese gardens, recognized the world over for their beauty and serenity.

JAPAN'S GARDENS

There are many different types of gardens in Japan, but all create an idealized landscape. Gardens in Japan feature bridges, lanterns, pruned trees, steps, and walkways, depending upon the design. Ponds can contain *koi*, which are brightly colored fish. Japanese gardeners select plants for their beauty in every season. Maple leaves provide brilliance in the fall, and evergreen trees and bamboo provide year-round greenery.

ZEN GARDENS

A garden made of sand and pebbles, with the sand raked in patterns, is called a Zen garden. These gardens are particularly restful because there is little to break a person's concentration. This type of garden is often attached to Zen Buddhist temples.

JAPANESE STROLLING GARDENS

The Japanese design strolling gardens with views that change depending upon where the person happens to be. Sometimes the walkways reveal hidden ponds or plants.

MAKE A MINIATURE
JAPANESE GARDEN

WHAT YOU NEED

- Pencil and paper
- Shallow tray
- Soil, gravel, pebbles, rocks, moss
- Small container
- Water
- Blue food coloring, optional
- Miniature plastic items like bridges or pagodas

WHAT TO DO

1. Sketch a design for your garden, planning where to place the materials you gathered.

2. Fill the shallow tray with a thin layer of soil; place the other materials where you wish. Gravel can represent rocks; rocks become mountains; moss can represent grass or fields. A small container filled with water becomes a pond. Add blue food coloring to the water, if you wish. Add a bridge or pagoda to your landscape. Take care not to place too many things in the landscape. Fewer things will create a more peaceful design.

TRIM AND CLIP

Bonsai originated in China over a thousand years ago, but Japan has taken it to new artistic heights. Bonsai gardeners continually prune normal trees to keep them tiny, trimming the roots as well as limbs to form the finished tree. Gardeners devote a lifetime to their trees, and the bonsai are bequeathed to the gardener's heir.

Say It!

bonsai (bohn-sah-ee)

ikebana (ee-keh-bah-nah)

A Japanese bonsai tree

FLOWER RULES

Buddhist priests brought the art of *ikebana,* or flower arrangement, to Japan. These artistic arrangements are based on combining natural materials. *Ikebana* has specific rules on how to place branches, leaves, buds, seed pods, fruit, and flowers. These arrangements are asymmetrical and even use empty space as part of the arrangement.

So What's Asymmetrical?

If something is *asymmetrical*, one side is not equal, or the same, as the corresponding side.

CREATE AN
IKEBANA ARRANGEMENT

WHAT YOU NEED

- Floral frog
- Shallow dish
- Flowers, open and budded
- Ferns
- Branches
- River stones

WHAT TO DO

1. Place the floral frog in the bottom of the dish and add water.

2. Choose your best flower with 1 blossom and some buds, and stick it into the frog.

3. Arrange the remaining flowers, ferns, and branches, choosing them one at a time as they fit.

4. Keep your arrangement simple, even if you do not use all of your flowers.

5. Arrange the river stones on the bottom of the dish.

Got Tea?

In Japan, serving tea is a ceremony called *sado*. It takes a person many years of study to master tea ceremony because each and every movement is ritualized. Those who practice tea ceremony in Japan appreciate the beauty and peacefulness of the moment, but some tea ceremonies can last up to four hours. Could you sit that long?

Say It!

cha-ire (chah-ee-reh)

chansen (chahn-sehn)

chawan (chah-wahn)

kama (kah-mah)

sado (sah-doh)

Tools of the Trade

The utensils used for a tea ceremony are very specific. Some of them are as follows:

kama—kettle for boiling the water
cha-ire—container to hold powdered green tea
chansen—bamboo whisk used to mix the tea
chawan—tea bowl, usually shared by guests

Tea Scholars

A Chinese Buddhist monk first introduced tea to Japan around the sixth century. The tea ceremony itself has its roots in Zen Buddhism, and the ceremony celebrates harmony, respect, purity, and tranquility. Some Japanese study *sado* many years in order to master it because each and every movement is a formal ritual.

HAVE A
TEA PARTY

WHAT YOU NEED

- 2 or more people
- 1 small teacup for each person
- Cookies
- Kettle
- Green tea leaves
- Teapot
- Small plates

WHAT TO DO

1. Invite your friends or family to join you for a tea party.

2. Straighten the table and the area around it. Remove everything not absolutely necessary; counters should be empty. Arrange cookies on small plates. Fill the kettle with water.

3. When your guests arrive, ask permission or help from an adult to put the kettle on to boil the water.

4. Invite your guests to sit at the table. Ask them to speak softly and only about happy things.

5. Place loose green tea leaves (about a teaspoon for every 8 ounces of water) into the teapot.

6. When the water begins to bubble but is not a full boil, pour hot water into the teapot. Set aside to steep for 1 to 2 minutes.

7. Place a teacup in front of each person and fill each halfway with tea. Pour your own last. Sit down and thank your guests for coming. Tell them a little about what you learned about the Japanese tea ceremony and explain that this is a very simplified version of it.

8. Invite your guests to sip the tea. Serve the cookies and guide the discussion. Make sure all guests feel included.

9. After everyone has finished the tea and cookies, remove the plates and cups. Thank your guests again for coming.

Folded Mysteries

Origami, invented by the Japanese, is the art of folding paper into various shapes. (Origami literally translated means "fold paper.") Some people think origami might have begun when paper shapes were used as decorations for Shinto ceremonies. During the Heian period (794–1185), paper was folded as decorative wrappings for letters and gifts. By the Tokugawa period (1603–1868), people were inventing creative ways of folding paper into fun shapes of animals, plants, and other things. Instructions for folding various shapes were not written down until 1797 but were handed down orally from generation to generation.

The crane (or *tsuru*) is the most popular origami, but it is perhaps one of the most complicated. There are, however, many origami that are easier to fold, such as goldfish.

A New Paper

Paper was introduced to Japan in 610 by a Buddhist monk from China. Japan quickly developed a new way of making paper, and by 800, Japan was known for their sturdy yet soft paper called *washi*. Most *washi* is made from *kozo* (mulberry) bark, a shrub which grows about ten feet in a year. In the winter, the *kozo* is harvested by cutting the stalks and bundled. The bark is made up of three layers: the black outer layer, the middle green layer, and the whiter inner layer. Most *washi* use only the white inner layer of bark.

Say It!

kozo (koh-zoh)

origami (oh-ree-gah-mee)

tsuru (tsoo-roo)

washi (wah-shee)

ORIGAMI GOLDFISH

WHAT YOU NEED

· Origami paper (or square paper)

WHAT TO DO

Note: The dotted lines indicate folds. Arrows indicate folding direction.

1. Place origami paper with color side down on a table. Fold paper in half, in a slightly crooked manner. (See figure 1.)

2. Bring the bottom left corner up to the top right corner and crease diagonally. (See figure 2.)

3. Fold the top right corner to the left, creasing the paper from A to B. (See figures 3 and 4.)

4. Flip over.

5. There's your goldfish! (See figure 5.)

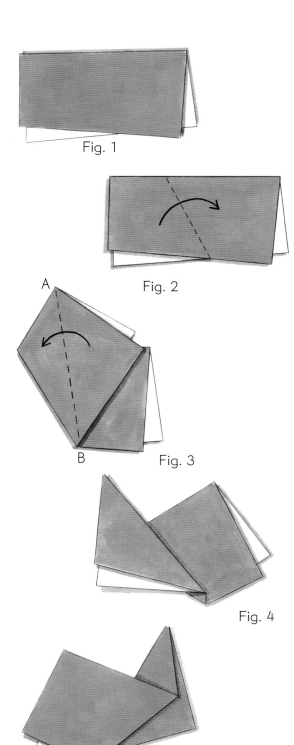

Fig. 1

Fig. 2

A
B
Fig. 3

Fig. 4

Fig. 5

A WISH FOR PEACE

In 1797, a book on origami was published entitled *Hiden Senbazuru Orikata* or *How to Fold a Thousand Cranes*. The crane is one of the most challenging and difficult creations ever produced by origami, but legend has it that if you can fold one thousand cranes, your prayers would be answered. No one knows how this idea began, but people around the world now know about it because of a twelve-year-old girl named Sadako Sasaki.

Sadako was two years old and living in Hiroshima with her family when the atom bomb was dropped on that city. Only a few years later, she fell ill with leukemia caused by the radiation from the bomb. Sadako began to fold paper cranes, hoping that 1,000 cranes could make her well. Before she could finish folding 1,000, she died, but her classmates finished folding the 1,000 cranes for her. Although Sadako lost her battle with leukemia at the age of twelve, her courage and hope inspired children all over Japan. They collected money to build a monument to Sadako. The monument was placed in Hiroshima Peace Park and depicts Sadako holding a folded crane high in the air. Even today, her courage and hope continue to inspire children all over the world in a desire to see the world live in peace.

Children's Peace Monument, Peace Memorial Park, Hiroshima, Japan

PONDER THIS

There is a statue of Sadako in a park in Seattle, Washington. Children from all over the world send *tsuru* (paper cranes) to the Sadako Peace Park in Seattle and to the Children's Peace Museum in Hiroshima, Japan, as a way to share the hope for world peace.

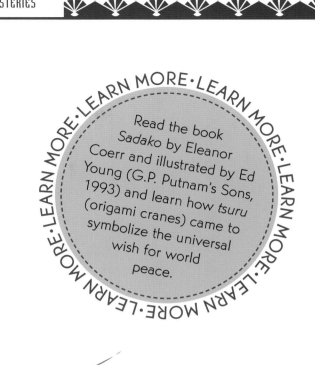

LEARN MORE·LEARN MORE·LEARN MORE·LEARN MORE·LEARN MORE·LEARN MORE·LEARN MORE·LEARN MORE·

Read the book *Sadako* by Eleanor Coerr and illustrated by Ed Young (G.P. Putnam's Sons, 1993) and learn how *tsuru* (origami cranes) came to symbolize the universal wish for world peace.

S.S. Crane

Mysteries of Art

Like everything else in Japan, the puppet shows, poems, and music may, at first, seem strange and mysterious to Western eyes and ears. The beauty of these arts, however, quickly becomes apparent; and people all over the world enjoy the special beauty of Japanese puppet shows, haiku poems, and serene music.

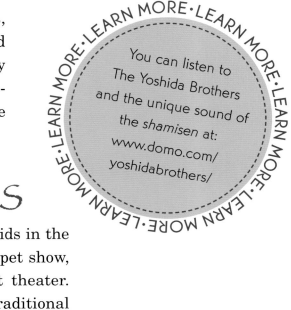

LEARN MORE·LEARN MORE·LEARN MORE·LEARN MORE·LEARN MORE·LEARN MORE·LEARN MORE·LEARN MORE·LEARN MORE

You can listen to The Yoshida Brothers and the unique sound of the shamisen at: www.domo.com/ yoshidabrothers/

MASTER PUPPETEERS

When you think of puppet shows, do you think of kids in the audience? In Japan, all ages enjoy a type of puppet show, called *bunraku*, which is Japanese traditional puppet theater. Bunraku began around 1600 as a combination of the traditional puppets, storytelling, and the music of the *shamisen*. Bunraku puppets are four feet tall, and it takes three people to control them. A master puppeteer moves the head and right arm; a second person works the left arm; and a third person controls the legs and feet.

During the puppet show, the master puppeteer is in plain sight, but the other two puppeteers wear black clothes and hoods, which allow them to blend into the background. The storyteller, or *tayu*, is also in plain sight. He tells the story while a musician, also in view, plays a stringed instrument called a *shamisen*. Most bunraku puppet shows are about history and can last up to ninety minutes.

Say It!

bunraku (boon-rah-koo)

haiku (hah-ee-koo)

shamisen (shah-mee-sehn)

tayu (tah-yoo)

A PUPPET SHOW

WHAT YOU NEED

- Paper and pencil or pen
- Puppets, dolls, or stuffed animals
- 1 or more persons to help
- Audience of family or friends

WHAT TO DO

1. Make up your own story or use a story that you already know.

2. Write out the story.

3. Decide on the parts. Who will be the narrator? Who will direct which puppet?

4. Practice the puppet show. Perform bunraku style, with the puppeteers in plain sight.

5. Perform for friends or family.

RULES OF A POEM

Haiku is a very short form of traditional poetry that developed in Japan during the Tokugawa period (1603–1868). Traditional haiku is usually about something in nature or a season, and the poem describes an image. It is always written in the present tense. Haiku is a poem of only three lines, and although it does not rhyme, there are strict rules. The first line must have five syllables, the second line seven syllables, and the last line five syllables. One of the most famous haiku poets was a samurai named Basho. To him, life and art were joined. Here is one of Basho's haiku:

> An old pond.
> A frog jumps in.
> The sound of water.

Because this haiku is translated from Japanese, the syllables do not match the 5-7-5 rule, but it does follow the rule in its original Japanese:

> *Furu ike ya*
> *Kawazu tobikomu*
> *Mizu no oto.*

WRITE HAIKU

WHAT YOU NEED

- Pen or pencil
- Paper

WHAT TO DO

1. Think of an animal, plant, tree, ocean or stream, or even a food you like.

2. Write a haiku about that subject. Use descriptive words.

3. Have 5 syllables in the first line.

4. Seven syllables in the second line.

5. And 5 syllables in the third and last line.

LEARN MORE·LEARN MORE·LEARN MORE·LEARN MORE·LEARN MORE·LEARN MORE·LEARN MORE·LEARN MORE·LEARN MORE·

There are many more kinds of arts the Japanese are famous for. Research others such as e-makimono (decorative scrolls that tell stories), calligraphy, ceramics, ukiyo-e (woodblock prints), and more.

EXAMPLES

My Dog (Title)

Trixie takes a walk. (5 syllables)

She sniffs grass, trees, rocks—a cat? (7 syllables)

Dog barks; cat runs fast. (5 syllables)

The Park (Title)

Giant redwood trees. (5 syllables)

Towering branches spread wide. (7 syllables)

Home to birds and bugs. (5 syllables)

THE MYSTERY OF MUSIC

The Japanese have some very unique instruments. Originally, many instruments in Japan came from China and could only be used by royalty and for religious rituals. As time went on, everyone in Japan was allowed to learn to play instruments and listen to music. Here are a few of Japan's unique instruments.

Fig. 1

Say It!

shamisen (shah-mee-sehn)

shakuhachi (shah-koo-hah-chee)

koto (koh-toh)

kotsuzumi (koh-tsu-zoo-mee)

KOTSUZUMI

The *kotsuzumi* is a small drum shaped like an hourglass. A sitting musician holds the drum against his right shoulder. With his right hand, he hits the drumhead while his left hand squeezes the cords to change the tone.

MAKE A KOTSUZUMI

WHAT YOU NEED

- Scissors
- Construction paper
- 1 empty cardboard oatmeal canister
- Markers
- Tape
- Yarn

WHAT TO DO

1. Cut construction paper to fit around the canister. Decorate the paper with the markers.

2. Remove lid. Tape the construction paper around the entire canister.

3. Tape the yarn along the sides of the canister in a zigzag pattern. (See figure 1.) Replace lid.

4. With your left hand, hold the drum against your right shoulder and hit the drum with your right hand.

KOTO

SHAKUHACHI

SHAMISEN

KOTO

The *koto* has thirteen strings and a boxy body. The musician places it on the floor or table and either kneels above it or sits in a chair. He or she plucks the strings with three picks, called *tsume*, worn on the thumb and first two fingers of the right hand. By pressing on the strings with the left hand, the tone changes.

SHAKUHACHI

A *shakuhachi* is a bamboo flute. The shakuhachi usually has four finger holes on the front and one on the back and comes in different lengths. Average length is about 1.8 feet (54.8 cm).

SHAMISEN

The *shamisen* is a three-stringed instrument from 3.5 to 4.5 feet (1.1–1.4 m) long. The musician uses a large pick, a *bachi*, to strike or pluck the strings. The shamisen is traditional in the bunraku theaters.

THE ART OF DOLLS

Dolls, or *ningyo* in Japanese, are an important part of Japanese culture, and not just on Girl's Day. There are two types of Japanese dolls that are renowned the world over as art objects. These are the whimsical wooden *Kokeshi* dolls and the exquisite hand-sculpted clay *Hakata* dolls. Each of these doll types come from a specific area in Japan that is known for its doll artists.

Say It!

ningyo (neen-gyoh)

Kokeshi (koh-keh-shee)

Hakata (hah-kah-tah)

IT'S NOT JUST WHITTLIN'!

Kokeshi dolls originally represented women and girls, although today male dolls are also available. These dolls are well known as a form of Japanese folk art. Kokeshi dolls are made of wood and have a simple design. Traditional Kokeshi dolls have no arms or legs, but their hand-painted faces express sweetness and humor. Artisans in Tohoku, in northern Honshu, create these dolls.

Kokeshi dolls

MOLDING MINIATURE PEOPLE

Hakata dolls are delicate dolls made of clay from the Hakata district of Fukuoka, a city on the island of Kyushu. The artisan sculpts the doll from pure white clay found only in the Fukuoka region. A plaster mold is then made of the figure, and copies of the original are formed. Each unglazed doll is fired and handpainted. Collectors consider these dolls fine art.

PONDER THIS

Every April in Tokyo, the newest Hakata dolls are unveiled in an exhibition.

MAKE A
KOKESHI DOLL

WHAT YOU NEED

- Newspapers
- 3 small square wooden blocks (available at craft stores)
- Wood glue
- Craft paints and paintbrush
- Markers
- 1 wooden "Doll's head" sphere with flat bottom

WHAT TO DO

1. Cover your work area with newspapers.

2. Stack 3 wooden blocks on top of each other for the doll's body. Glue the wooden blocks together. Set aside to dry according to wood glue instructions.

3. Using markers and/or paints, draw the doll's face and hair on the head. (See figure 1.)

4. Using markers and/or paints, draw a kimono on the body. You can be as simple or elaborate as you want.

5. After the paints or markers have dried, glue the head of the doll to the body.

Try It!

After you practice making your traditional Kokeshi doll, try making your family as Kokeshi dolls. Change the hairstyle for boys and dads. Paint happi coats on the children in your family, or even blue jeans and t-shirts. They might not be traditional Japanese Kokeshi dolls, but you can have some fun with these simple, yet sweet, dolls.

Fig. 1

History's Mysteries

Little is known about Japan's history before the fifth century, because until then, Japan did not have a written language. Most of what is known about Japan before A.D. 400 comes from archaeological discoveries and written accounts from other countries, especially from China. Many archaeologists think that during the ice ages, when the sea level was low, Japan's first inhabitants probably walked from Siberia, China, Korea, or the Okinawa islands. As the earth warmed, the sea rose and separated Japan into islands.

JOMON PERIOD 14,500 B.C.–300 B.C.

Archaeologists discovered pottery from more than 40,000 years ago and named this earliest period *Jomon* after the unique cord pattern found on the pottery. Shells and crude tools have been unearthed that indicate the people from this era hunted, fished, and gathered plants for their food.

SO WHAT'S AN ARCHAEOLOGIST?

An *archaeologist* is a person who studies items from the past in order to learn about the origins of peoples and their culture.

MAKE A
TIME CAPSULE

WHAT YOU NEED

- A box with a lid, like a shoebox
- Markers
- Tape

WHAT TO DO

1. Decorate the sides of the box with markers, drawing some of your favorite things, like movie characters, pets, or foods. (See figure 1.)

2. Place items into the box that mean a lot to you, but nothing that is worth a lot of money. For instance, if you love playing tennis, place a tennis ball into the box. If your favorite animal is a duck, place a picture or a figurine of a duck into the box. Do not place anything into the box that is valuable, perishable, or something you will need.

3. Seal the box with tape.

4. Calculate what year it will be in 5 years and write "Do Not Open Until (Date)."

5. Put the box somewhere for safekeeping, like in your closet.

6. When the date arrives, open the time capsule and enjoy rediscovering what you liked when you were five years younger.

Try It!

Interview your parents about your birth and ask for stories about what you were like as an infant and toddler. Write down the stories in a journal. You can start keeping a daily account, like a diary, or just write in it when something important or special happens. Make sure to write down the dates.

Say It!

Jomon (joh-mohn)

Fig. 1

YAYOI PERIOD 300 B.C.—A.D. 300

Archaeologists believe that people from China and Korea moved into Japan during this period and pushed the Jomon north. The new settlers brought rice, bronze, and iron. They built homes of wood with thatched roofs and dirt floors, and they fashioned weapons, such as swords and spears, from iron and bronze. Archaeologists named this period *Yayoi* after the Tokyo street where fragments of pottery from the era were discovered.

PONDER THIS

What are the advantages of living in a tribe that moved around all the time? What are the advantages of living in a settlement?

KOFUN PERIOD 300–600

Huge tombs, called *kofun,* were built between the third and seventh centuries for the burial of kings and other powerful clan leaders and gave this period its name. Many of these tombs have not yet been explored, but the largest tomb measured is longer than five football fields. Although some of the tombs are square or circular, most are keyhole shaped. Kofun building ended with the introduction of Buddhism.

A PERSONAL AIR CONDITIONER

Ancient Romans, Greeks, and Chinese made fans of leaves, wood, feathers, and linen stretched over wooden slats. In the eighth century, the Japanese invented a folding fan. It was carried by both men and women.

Say It!

Kofun (koh-foon)

Yayoi (yah-yoh-ee)

MAKE A JAPANESE
FOLDING FAN

WHAT YOU NEED

- Construction paper
- Markers
- Stapler

WHAT TO DO

1. Draw a colorful design or picture on your construction paper. (See figure 1.)

2. Fold the bottom edge of one short side up about one inch. (See figure 2.)

3. Flip the page over so that the fold is on top and away from you. (See figure 3.) Fold the top edge down the same size as your first fold. (See figure 4.)

4. Continue flipping and folding until the entire paper is folded into one narrow strip.

5. Staple the folds together about one inch from the bottom. Open the top folds to open your fan. (See figure 5.)

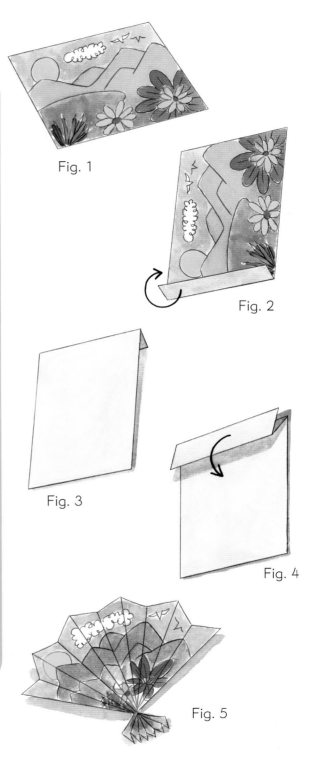

Fig. 1

Fig. 2

Fig. 3

Fig. 4

Fig. 5

YAMATO PERIOD 400–700

The name of this era came from the location of the emperor's court on the "Yamato Plain," near present-day Osaka. This period marked the beginning of the sun goddess mythology from which all later emperors of Japan claimed divine ancestry. The Yamato period also formalized the Shinto religion. During this time, Japan adopted much from China, including Buddhism and Confucianism, the Chinese calendar, and China's written language.

HAKUHO PERIOD 645–710

During the Hakuho Period, government began to be centralized under one emperor; and in 702, the government developed the Taiho code. This code outlined the duties for government officials, laws for citizens to follow, and punishment for criminals.

NARA PERIOD 710–794

In 710 the Japanese capital was established in Nara, giving the period its name. Most of the people followed Shinto beliefs, but Emperor Shomu embraced Buddhism. From this time on, a gradual combination of Buddhism and Shinto took place. This era also saw the spread of written language, and Japan's first histories were written. Landowners hired samurai to protect their property.

Say It!

Heian (hey-ee-ahn)

Hakuho (hah-koo-hoh)

kana (kah-nah)

Kyoto (kyo-toh)

Nara (nah-rah)

wako (wah-koh)

Yamato (yah-mah-toh)

CLAP
CLAP

HEIAN PERIOD 794–1185

The capital moved again—to Heian (today's Kyoto) and gave this period its name. A simplified written alphabet, called *kana,* was introduced, and art and literature flourished. *Wako* (pirates) ruled the seas, and landowners fought each other, leading them to hire samurai. After 1100, two powerful clans began struggling for power: the Taira in the west, who had defeated the wako, and the Minamoto in the east. In 1192 the first *shogunate* was established at Kamakura by the Minamoto clan.

"ONE WHO SERVES"

The Heian government established a military system of hired soldiers, called samurai, literally meaning "one who serves." Originally, they owed loyalty to the emperor, but this changed to loyalty to the landowners. For almost a thousand years, Japan's military consisted of soldiers in countless private armies, all of whom owed their loyalty to the local warlords.

SO WHAT'S A SAMURAI?

Literally translated, *samurai* means "one who serves." Samurai were hired soldiers.

MYSTERY OF THE SHOGUN

For nearly 700 years, shoguns and their governments, known as *shogunates*, ruled Japan, and emperors were powerless. The shogun was the real head of the government, and they forced the emperor to issue imperial decrees. If the emperors tried to regain authority, they were defeated. By 1185 the emperor's only job was to appoint shoguns and show up for ceremonies. For the next 700 years, real power was held by the shogun.

Say It!

Ashikaga (ah-shee-kah-gah)

Kamakura (kah-mah-koo-rah)

kamikaze (kah-mee-kah-zeh)

samurai (sah-moo-rah-ee)

shogun (shoh-goon)

KAMAKURA PERIOD 1185–1333

The Kamakura Period was the dawn of feudal Japan, when the military leaders—the shoguns— grew stronger and the emperor's power lessened. The first military ruler, Minamoto Yorimoto, was formally appointed by the court as shogun in 1192. Through the services of the samurai, military power was vested locally in the landowners. The constant wars of this period weakened the shogun and allowed the Ashikaga clan, led by Takauji, to topple the Kamakura shogunate and rise to power.

A Divine Wind

In 1274 Mongols, led by Kublai Khan, invaded Japan. More than 900 ships carried 25,000 Mongols and Korean troops with catapults, bows, and arrows. The foreigners attacked the samurai, but after only one day of fighting, extremely bad weather turned back the invaders.

In 1281 Kublai Khan launched a second invasion with 150,000 Chinese, Mongols, and Koreans, and 40,000 ships. After seven weeks of fighting, a typhoon struck which destroyed the invaders. The Japanese gave credit to a divine wind (*kamikaze*) for protecting them.

Muromachi Period 1333–1573

When the Ashikaga family came into power, Ashikaga Takuji was a weak shogun, and Japan split into northern and southern territories, each at war with the other. The local warlords became so powerful that they created their own laws. Japan was in chaos, but trade continued to flourish, and from China came bonsai, ikebana, and the tea ceremony.

FEUDAL JAPAN

During the feudal period, Japan had rigid classes. At top was the shogun, then the *daimyo*. Next were samurai, farmers, craftspeople, and merchants. Some groups did not fit into a class, such as actors and priests. On the very bottom were the *eta,* who butchered animals, tanned hides, and did any job associated with death. Since status was inherited, eta were shunned from birth to death.

Try It!

Mon is a crest and *kamon* is a specific family crest in Japan. Each family has a crest that is carried down through the generations. The chrysanthemum is the kamon for the emperor. Other family crests are the butterfly, moon, bamboo, and fan. Does your family have a crest? Do some research to find out. Or make your own crest.

LEARN MORE • LEARN MORE • LEARN MORE • LEARN MORE • LEARN MORE • LEARN MORE • LEARN MORE

See some kamon of famous historical Japanese people at www.asgy.co.jp/ anglais/famous/ famous.html

SO WHAT'S A DAIMYO?

Daimyos governed a domain, which was an area of land assigned to him by the shogunate.

HERE COME THE EUROPEANS

During the Muromachi period, Japan began trading with Europe. In 1542 the Portuguese arrived in Japan and introduced firearms. The Spanish followed in 1587, and the Dutch arrived later, in 1600. Japan imported silks, porcelain, art, and tobacco, while exporting gold, pearls, swords, and lumber. Although there were turmoil and conflict within Japan, feudal lords (daimyo) became rich and powerful through trade. In 1549 the Jesuit priest Francis Xavier arrived in Japan, and other missionaries soon followed.

THE SAMURAI

In the tenth century, samurai were recruited to fight invaders. The samurai developed an ornate battle-dress including two swords. They dressed in a *kataginu* (outer jacket) and *hakama* (pants). Over this was a kimono with their *kamon* (family crest) on the back. Armor included an ornate helmet, a mask to protect the face, coverings for shoulders, arms, legs, and even shin guards. Samurai warriors took great care with their hair. Before going into battle, samurai warriors shaved the tops of their heads. When not wearing helmets, they pulled the side and back hair into a topknot, called a *chomage*. It would be considered a loss of face if their hair fell down during a fight or if someone cut it off. In the 1870s, the samurai class was eliminated and their privileged status revoked.

Say It!

bushido (buh-shee-doh)

chomage (choh-mah-geh)

hakama (hah-kah-mah)

kamon (kah-mohn)

kataginu (kah-tah-ghee-noo)

Muromachi (moo-roh-mah-chee)

BUSHIDO

The samurai were bound by a strict code of behavior and loyalty, called *bushido*. If the samurai died by his own hand, it was considered a brave end as opposed to the humiliation of a defeat at the hands of the enemy.

PONDER THIS

Only the samurai could have a family name and a first name.

A United Japan

After the chaos of invaders, local warlords creating their own laws, and weak shoguns who could not rule the country, three strong warlords came to power and finally unified Japan. Their methods, however, were often brutal.

Azuchi-Momoyama Period 1574–1600

Oda Nobunaga, whose goal was to unite Japan under "a single sword," rose to power in 1568. He destroyed the Buddhist monastery of Mount Hiei (in Kyoto) and killed the monks who for years had fought against the shogun. Nobunaga welcomed the Europeans with their firearms, which gave him power and political strength. When he covered his battleships with iron, his navy became indestructible. Nobunaga was assassinated in 1582, and Toyotomi Hideyoshi became shogun.

Hideyoshi disarmed all non-samurai; and by 1590, he had successfully unified Japan. Hideyoshi invaded Korea in an attempt to conquer China, slaughtering thousands of Koreans and Chinese. In 1598 Toyotomi Hideyoshi died. The final unification of Japan would fall to the third great hero of Japanese history, Tokugawa Ieyasu.

Say It!

Hakodate (hah-koh-dah-teh)

Hiei (hee-eh-ee)

Oda Nobunaga (oh-dah noh-boo-nah-gah)

Shimoda (shee-moh-dah)

Tokugawa Ieyasu (toh-koo-gah-wah ee-eh-yah-soo)

Toyotomi Hideyoshi (toh-yoh-toh-mee hee-deh-yoh-shee)

TOKUGAWA OR EDO PERIOD 1603–1868

When Tokugawa Ieyasu became shogun in 1603, he moved his headquarters to Edo (today's Tokyo) while the emperor remained in Heian. Tokugawa closed the country to outsiders and prohibited citizens and rescued shipwrecked foreign sailors from leaving Japan. Christian missionaries, who had been in Japan since the early 1500s, were thrown out of the country, and Christianity was no longer recognized as a religion in Japan. Scientific books from Europe were banned, and all foreign-born people were deported. The country began a period of isolation as trade with the outside world came to an end. Japan remained isolated until 1853, when U.S. Commodore Matthew Perry sailed into Tokyo Bay.

OPENING JAPAN

On July 8, 1853, Commodore Perry led a squadron of four U.S. ships into Tokyo Bay and presented representatives of the emperor with a proposed commercial and friendship treaty. The treaty, signed on March 31, 1854, provided that shipwrecked sailors be allowed to return home, U.S. ships be permitted to buy coal in Japan, and the ports of Shimoda and Hakodate be opened to U.S. commerce. Perry's mission ended Japan's long isolation.

CASTLES OF WOOD

After the warlord Oda Nobunaga and his successor Toyotomi Hideyoshi finally united all Japan, the resulting peace brought an age of magnificent castle building. The castles were built of stone and wood, but few remain.

Say It!

Himeji (hee-meh-jee)

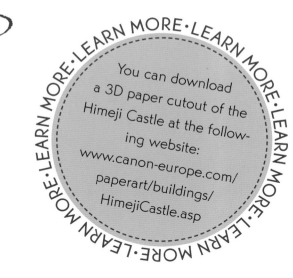

You can download a 3D paper cutout of the Himeji Castle at the following website:
www.canon-europe.com/paperart/buildings/HimejiCastle.asp

LEARN MORE·LEARN MORE·LEARN MORE·LEARN MORE·LEARN MORE·LEARN MORE·LEARN MORE·LEARN MORE·

JAPANESE CASTLES

Powerful landlords, or daimyo, built large, elaborate castles not only as protection but also to impress their rivals and subjects. At the center of the fortress stood a multi-storied tower where the daimyo lived surrounded by his samurai. Rings of moats, stone walls, and watchtowers surrounded and protected the castle tower. These rings helped slow down enemies as they zigzagged from gate to gate to reach the inner castle. It was like a giant maze, and paths sometimes led to a dead end. Windows in the walls allowed defenders to shoot arrows at attackers from above.

DESIGN A
FORTRESS

WHAT YOU NEED

- Paper and pencil
- Markers
- Poster board

WHAT TO DO

1. Using the paper and pencil, sketch a design for your castle fortress. Think about the materials you would use to build it. Where would you build your castle? On a mountain? In a valley? Near a forest? By a river? How would you protect it from enemies? Where would you store weapons? Would there be a moat? What kind of doors?

2. Using markers and the poster board, draw your fortress design. Include a key—a list of explanations for symbols used in your drawing. For example, you might use a square with an X through it for a door and explain this in your key.

THE WHITE HERON

One of the few castles still remaining in its original form is Himeji Castle. The castle is covered with white plaster which, at the time, fireproofed the castle. The castle is built of wood, so fireproofing was very important. The Himeji Castle is nicknamed the "White Heron."

MEIJI PERIOD 1868–1912

Emperor Meiji was only fifteen when he took the throne. He eliminated the samurai and daimyo, thus ending the shogun era. He moved the capital from Heian to Edo and renamed the city Tokyo, today's capital. Emperor Meiji built up the military in order to increase Japan's land. He attacked China, resulting in the Sino-Japanese War (1894–1895). After defeating China, Japan controlled Taiwan. In 1904 Japan defeated Russia in a war over Korea and Manchuria; and in 1910 Japan annexed Korea. By the time of the emperor's death in 1912, Japan had a constitution, political parties, a prime minister, and a parliament called the *Diet*.

TAISHO PERIOD 1912–1926

Upon the death of Emperor Meiji, his son Taisho came to power determined to increase Japan's territory. World War I was raging in Europe. Japan declared war on Germany and moved into China and the Pacific islands controlled by Germany. At the World War I peace conference at Versailles, Japan was awarded the Pacific islands it had seized.

Say It!

Akihito (ah-kee-hee-toh)

Hirohito (hee-roh-hee-toh)

Heisei (hey-ee-seh-ee)

Meiji (meh-ee-jee)

Showa (shoh-wah)

Taisho (tah-ee-shoh)

SHOWA PERIOD 1926–1989

After Emperor Taisho's death, his son Hirohito ascended the throne as emperor. The Showa Period can be divided into three sub-periods: expansion, occupation, and post-occupation. Emperor Hirohito continued to build up his military with an eye to expanding his territory. By 1936 Japan was a fascist country and signed a treaty with another fascist country: Hitler's Germany. Japan's army conquered Manchuria, parts of China—including Shanghai and Nanking—Korea, Singapore, and many Pacific islands. On December 7, 1941, the Japanese attacked the United States' naval fleet at Pearl Harbor, Hawaii, forcing the U.S. to declare war on Japan.

HEISEI PERIOD 1989–PRESENT

After Emperor Hirohito's death in 1989, his oldest son, Akihito, took the throne. His reign has been designated Heisei, or "Achieving Peace." Akihito is the first emperor in Japan's history who has never been proclaimed a direct descendant of the sun goddess. Instead, the constitution of Japan states that the emperor is "the symbol of the State and of the unity of the people" and derives his position from "the will of the people with whom resides sovereign power."

SO WHAT'S FASCISM?

Fascism is a form of government that is extremely nationalistic and believes in the supremacy of one ethnic group and obedience to one powerful leader.

A DEADLY WIND

I n an effort to end World War II, the U.S. dropped the first atomic bomb on Hiroshima, Japan, on August 6, 1945. Emperor Hirohito refused to surrender. Three days later, the U.S. dropped another atomic bomb, this time on Nagasaki. The emperor surrendered, bringing World War II to an end. It is impossible to determine how many Japanese died in the bombings, although estimates are that 70,000 in Hiroshima and 74,000 in Nagasaki died instantly, with many more deaths later due to radiation sickness and cancer. Japan lost over 3.1 million people as a result of the war.

LEARN MORE·LEARN MORE·LEARN MORE·LEARN MORE·LEARN MORE·LEARN MORE·LEARN MORE·LEARN MORE·

A Peace Memorial Museum in Hiroshima was built in 1955 to help everyone remember the devastating effects of the atom bomb and to promote peace throughout the world. See the Kid's Page from the museum: www.pcf.city.hiroshima.jp/kids/KPSH_E/top_e.html

OCCUPATION

After the defeat of Japan in World War II, the U.S. military, under the command of General Douglas MacArthur, occupied Japan. Occupation lasted until 1952, during which time Japan returned all territory seized during the war. Emperor Hirohito remained on the throne, but no longer had divine status. The emperor was now only the symbolic head of government. The parliament and prime minister, all elected, actually ran Japan. The occupation was a time for rebuilding cities, factories, and homes. A formal peace treaty, the San Francisco Treaty, was signed on September 8, 1951, and Japan regained its sovereignty.

THE POST-OCCUPATION OF JAPAN

The years since 1952 have seen an explosion of growth in manufacturing and exports in Japan. Through international cooperation and peaceful methods, Japan has once again become a world power, but this time in economics and trade.

Food Mysteries

What do you think of when you think of food in Japan? Sushi? Rice? Ramen? Much of what is Japanese cuisine actually originated in China, but the Japanese adapted the foods to make them their own. One of the things unique to Japan is that they serve their meals on separate little dishes. A dinner could consist of four or more small dishes for each person.

Say It!

gochisosama (goh-chee-soh-sah-mah)

itadakimasu (ee-tah-dah-kee-mah-soo)

mochiko (moh-chee-koh)

katakuriko (kah-tah-koo-ree-koh)

Japanese Table Manners

ALWAYS...

Say *itadakimasu* before eating to thank the host.

Slurp your noodles.

Drink your soup. Hold the bowl with your thumb on the rim and four fingers on the bottom.

Hold the rice bowl the same way as the soup bowl.

When finished, say *gochisosama* to thank the host.

NEVER...

Point or play with chopsticks.

Leave food on your plate.

Spear food with chopsticks. To take food from a serving plate, turn chopsticks around and use the thicker end.

Burp or blow your nose at the table.

78

MICROWAVE MOCHI

WHAT YOU NEED

- 1½ cup *mochiko* (Japanese rice flour)
- 1 cup sugar
- 1½ cup water
- 8-inch square microwave-safe dish
- Cooking spray
- *Katakuriko* (potato starch)
- Knife
- Cutting board
- Sugar and cinnamon, optional

Note: Both mochiko and katakuriko can be purchased in an Asian grocery store.

WHAT TO DO

1. In a large bowl, combine mochiko, sugar, and water. Mix until smooth.

2. Spray microwave-safe dish with cooking spray. Pour mixture into dish. Microwave on high for 7½ minutes.

3. Dust the cutting board with katakuriko.

4. With an adult's help and using potholders or oven mitts, carefully remove the dish from the microwave. *Caution, it will be hot.* Flip dish upside down on the cutting board. Mochi will come out in a big square.

5. Let mochi cool thoroughly.

6. Cut into 16 2-inch squares. Serve as is or dip for extra flavor. To dip, moisten slightly with water then dip into sugar or a cinnamon-sugar mixture.

Magic Beans

Soybeans are a very important part of the Japanese cuisine, and they come in various forms. Soybeans are high in protein and B vitamins. These beans can be curdled for tofu, roasted for snacks, used instead of meat, and even soaked, ground, and strained for nutritious soy milk.

Edamame

Edamame are green soybeans served shelled for a side dish or in the pod as a tasty snack. To eat, place the pod between your teeth and squeeze so the beans will pop out. Eat the beans and throw away the pod. As a snack, edamame can be roasted.

Soy Sauce

Soy sauce, *shoyu*, is a salty, dark liquid made from fermented soybeans. It is used both in cooking and as a table seasoning. A shoyu bottle is on every table in Japan.

Miso

Miso is a rich, salty, thick paste made from fermented soybeans and used to flavor many dishes, such as soups and salad dressings.

Tofu

Tofu is curdled soybean milk pressed into blocks. Tofu has little taste of its own but takes on the flavors of additives. It makes a good substitute for meat or cheese and is a delicious addition to salads and soups.

OMSUBI SANDWICH

WHAT YOU NEED

- Hot dog, ham, or bologna
- Pickled vegetable, optional
- 2 cups Japanese, or short-grain, rice
- 2½ cups water
- Large bowl
- Medium-sized saucepan
- Salt
- *Nori* (dried seaweed)

WHAT TO DO

1. With permission or help from an adult, chop meat and vegetables into small pieces and set aside.

2. Place rice into bowl and rinse until water runs clear. Drain.

3. In the saucepan, combine rice and 2½ cups of water; set aside for 30 minutes.

4. Cover saucepan and, with permission or help from an adult, cook rice according to package directions. Remove pan from heat; set aside for 15 minutes.

5. With a wooden spoon or rice paddle, gently turn rice to mix and fluff. Let cool.

6. Wet your hands with water; sprinkle salt on them. Form a ball with a handful of rice; form a depression in the center.

7. Drop a teaspoon of meat and vegetables into the center. Mold rice around the filling.

8. Cut a rectangle of nori and wrap around the rice ball.

RAW FISH—YUM

Sushi is vinegar-flavored rice topped with, or wrapped around, fish and other food items, such as pickles or vegetables. Some sushi have a strip of seaweed around the outside of the roll. Sushi is served on a large plate or wooden board accompanied by soy sauce, wasabi, and pickled ginger. To eat, mix a small amount of wasabi with soy sauce then lightly dip the sushi into it. Eat in one bite. Cleanse your palate with pickled ginger. If you wish to try sushi, begin by trying cooked sushi like *tamago* or the Americanized California roll that contains cooked crab, avocado, and cucumber.

Some of the most common sushi ingredients are:

maguro (mah-goo-roh) raw tuna

tobiko (toh-bee-koh) raw flying fish eggs

hamachi (hah-mah-chee) raw yellowtail

uni (oo-nee) raw sea urchin

unagi (oo-nah-ghee) grilled eel

tako (tah-koh) cooked octopus

tamago (tah-mah-goh) Japanese omelet

Say It!

dashi (dah-shee)

kombu (kohm-boo)

nori (noh-ree)

sushi (soo-shee)

sashimi (sah-shee-mee)

Tsukiji (tsoo-kee-jee)

wakame (wah-kah-meh)

So What's Wasabi?

Wasabi is made from the root of horseradish that is grated and mixed with water to form a paste. Wasabi has a strong, hot flavor.

SASHIMI

Sashimi is thinly sliced, raw fish or seafood served without rice. Sashimi is dipped into soy sauce and, depending on the kind of sashimi, wasabi or ground ginger can be mixed into the soy sauce.

Seaweed & Other Things

Japanese use *nori*—dried, thin sheets of seaweed—to wrap around rice or use in soups. *Wakame* is another type of seaweed—or kelp—that is wet and slimy in texture but delicious in soups and salads. *Kombu*—another seaweed—is used to make *dashi*, which is a broth made of kombu and dried fish and forms the base for many soups.

LEARN MORE · LEARN MORE · LEARN MORE · LEARN MORE · LEARN MORE · LEARN MORE · LEARN MORE · LEARN MORE

Read the picture book *The Wakame Gatherers* by Holly Thompson and illustrated by Kazumi Wilds (Shen's Books, 2007) to learn how wakame is harvested. The wonderful illustrations depict a seaside town in Japan.

NO DIVING

Ponder This

The Tsukiji market in Tokyo is the largest fish market in the world, taking in over 2,800 tons of fish a day. Tuna (maguro) comes from as far away as New Zealand. Because most sushi and sashimi are eaten raw, the Japanese market seeks only the best quality tuna.

Try It!

Find nori in the Asian food section of most big markets or in health food stores. Try a piece, either wrapped around a rice ball, *omusubi*, or plain. Some *nori* comes flavored. What does it taste like? Do you like it?

OODLES OF NOODLES

Since their introduction in the ninth century, noodles have become an important part of Japanese cuisine. There are white, thick noodles, called *udon*, thin ramen noodles from China, and *soba* noodles, made from buckwheat. There are even restaurants in Japan that serve only noodles.

BUCKWHEAT PASTA

Soba is a Japanese noodle made from buckwheat and is the size of spaghetti, only darker in color. Soba are eaten either hot or cold. If cold, soba can be dipped into soy sauce before being slurped up. Soba noodles can have many different kinds of toppings. Soba are so popular that Japanese soba restaurants compete for "best soba" award.

THICK PASTA

Udon are thick, white noodles made from wheat flour. They can be served in a hot broth with mushrooms or chicken or eaten cold with a dipping sauce. As with the other noodles, udon can be served with many types of toppings.

RAMEN NOODLES

Ramen are egg noodles served in a soup made of soy sauce, miso, or salt broth. Other items can be added, like shrimp or chicken, for a hearty meal.

Try It!

Ramen can be found in the soup section of your grocery store. The noodles come dried in a square block. Follow the instructions and then add your own toppings to make your ramen special. Try adding slices of cooked chicken or pork, cooked vegetables, or a sliced hard-boiled egg.

COLD SOBA NOODLES
WITH DIPPING SAUCE

WHAT YOU NEED

- 6-ounce package soba noodles
- ½ cup soy sauce
- ½ cup rice vinegar
- 1 tablespoon minced garlic
- 1 tablespoon thinly sliced scallions
- 1½ teaspoons chopped fresh ginger
- 2 teaspoons toasted sesame oil
- 1 teaspoon honey
- 1 teaspoon toasted sesame seeds

WHAT TO DO

Get permission or help from a grownup and cook noodles according to package directions. Drain in a colander and rinse in cold water. Add ice cubes to chill. In a small bowl, whisk together remaining ingredients. Dip cold, drained noodles into sauce and slurp.

Say It!

ramen (rah-mehn)

udon (oo-dohn)

soba (soh-bah)

PONDER THIS

In Yokohama, Japan, there is a large museum dedicated only to ramen. Displays of ramen packages, ramen bowls, and the history of ramen fill the museum. There's also a replica of an old-fashioned Japanese street with ramen restaurants.

JAPANESE TAKEOUT

A Japanese lunchbox with compartments is called a *bento box* and is sort of like a lunchbox. Traditional bento boxes are made of lacquered wood, although today some are disposable. A bento box lunch contains rice; vegetables, such as pickled Japanese radish or pumpkin (*kabocha*); and meat, such as fish or deep-fried pork cutlet (*tonkatsu*). Garnishes included might be pickled plums (*umeboshi*) or seaweed.

Say It!

hashi (hah-shee)

kabocha (kah-boh-chah)

tonkatsu (tohn-kah-tsoo)

umeboshi (oo-meh-boh-shee)

TEMPURA

Tempura is a light batter into which seafood such as prawns or vegetable slices are dipped before being deep-fried in very hot oil. Tempura is not greasy, because the high heat of the oil cooks it so quickly. The process of making tempura was probably introduced to Japan by Portuguese traders.

EAT WITH
CHOPSTICKS

WHAT YOU NEED

- Pair of chopsticks
- Cooked hot dog slices

WHAT TO DO

1. Rest one chopstick across the crook of your thumb and on your ring finger. Use your middle finger to hold it steady.

2. Grasp the other chopstick between your middle finger and your pointer finger. This is the upper stick. Use your thumb to hold it steady. (See figure 1.)

3. Move the upper stick up and down so that the tip comes together with the tip of the other chopstick. The lower chopstick should not move. (See figure 2.)

4. Use your chopsticks to pick up a piece of hot dog and eat it. This might take you several tries.

5. Try using your chopsticks to eat other things. Can you eat your dinner with chopsticks? (Cut up large pieces of meat before picking up with chopsticks.)

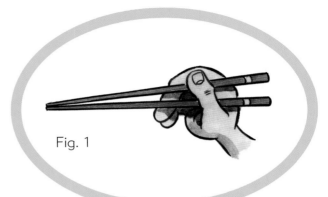

Fig. 1

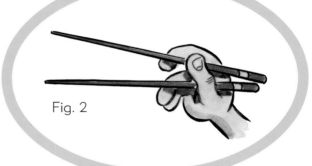

Fig. 2

CHOPSTICKS

Chopsticks, called *hashi* by the Japanese, were introduced to Japan by the Chinese around A.D. 500, but Japan made their chopsticks shorter and pointed. Japanese *hashi* are seven inches long for women and eight inches long for men. Chopsticks are usually made from wood, and the Japanese were the first to lacquer chopsticks. They invented disposable chopsticks in the late 1800s.

Mysterious Animals of Japan

Japan has some very unusual animals. There are monkeys that live in the snow and bathe in hot springs, graceful red-crowned cranes that dance for the joy of it, and the funny little raccoon dog. Let's take a closer look at Japan's mysterious animals.

RACCOON DOG

The Japanese raccoon dog gets its name from the dark "mask" on its face which makes it look like a raccoon, although it belongs to the dog family. Raccoon dogs are mostly nocturnal and will eat just about anything, including eggs, plants, insects, rodents, amphibians, and birds. They can swim, so they also eat fish, crab, and shellfish. Scientists believe the raccoon dogs have poor vision and have to rely on their sense of smell to find food.

ALL ABOUT THE RACCOON DOG

- Range: Europe, Russia, China, and Japan
- Habitat: lowlands, forests, and mountain valleys
- Diet: rodents, berries, insects, fruit, slugs, snails, fish, and crabs
- Weight: 8 to 22 pounds (4 to 10 kg)
- Length: 1.6 to 2.2 feet (50 to 68 cm)
- Tail length: 5 to 10 inches (13 to 25 cm)

SMELL-A-THON

WHAT YOU NEED

- 1 tablespoon cinnamon
- 1 tablespoon dirt
- 1 tablespoon vanilla extract
- 1 fragrant flower, such as a rose, separated into petals
- 1 tablespoon apple juice
- 1 tablespoon wood shavings
- 1 tablespoon lemon juice
- 1 tablespoon mint leaves
- 1 clean container with lid for each item above
- At least 1 other person
- Blindfold

WHAT TO DO

1. Place each of the first 8 items in separate containers. Cover each with a lid

2. Blindfold a friend.

3. Open the lid of one container and hold under your friend's nose. Ask him or her to sniff and try to identify the smell.

4. Replace lid and open the next container. Continue with all containers.

How many items did your friend identify? Would he or she survive as an animal that needed to rely upon smell to find food, as a raccoon dog does?

RED-CROWNED CRANE

The Japanese consider the red-crowned crane (*tancho* in Japanese) a symbol of longevity and success because of its graceful appearance and a legend that cranes live for a thousand years. Pairs have elaborate courtship dances with high leaps, bows, and wing stretches, then they sing a duet. After they build their nest on the ground with grasses and reeds, the female lays two eggs. Both the male and the female take care of the eggs and the chicks after hatching. The crane is almost all white with black feathers on the wings and neck and a patch of red skin on the forehead and crown.

Say It!

tancho (tahn-choh)

Ponder This

Adaptations are ways in which an animal is suited for its habitat. For example, a duck is suited to living on the water because of its webbed feet. A hawk is suited for eating rodents because of its strong curved beak. Think about what makes a crane perfect for living in the wetlands and for eating the type of food it eats.

ALL ABOUT THE RED-CROWNED CRANE:

- Range: permanent population in Hokkaido, Japan; migratory population winters in China and Korea, breeds in China and Russia
- Habitat: open marshes, bogs, and wetlands
- Diet: fish, amphibians, aquatic invertebrates, rodents, plants, and grain
- Weight: 17 to 22 pounds (7.7 to 9.9 kg)
- Height: 5 feet (1.52 m); wingspan up to 8 feet (2.4 m)

Help Your Animal Friends

There are many ways you can help protect wildlife populations. See if you can think of even more ways.

1. Have a fundraiser to donate money to a local or national organization that helps wildlife, like the World Wildlife Fund (http://www.worldwildlife.org/) or The Nature Conservancy (http://www.nature.org/).

2. Go to your local zoo and learn about the endangered animals there. Find out if there is a volunteer program for kids.

3. Throw your trash into the proper bins and not on the ground or in the water.

4. Recycle and compost.

PONDER THIS

Because of the lifetime bond between crane mates, they are often used as wedding symbols.

ENDANGERED!

Both the Japanese macaque and the red-crowned crane populations are in danger of disappearing in the wild. Why? Mostly because of habitat loss. As human populations grow, towns and farms encroach upon animal homes and their food supplies. The red-crowned crane population is estimated at fewer than 2,000.

YOUR NEW HOME

STELLER'S SEA EAGLE

The Steller's sea eagle is the world's heaviest known eagle. It breeds on the coasts of northeastern Russia and surrounding islands, but in the winter, it migrates to Japan.

Steller's eagles perch on a branch and watch the water. When they see a fish, they swoop down on the prey, dip their feet into the water, and grab their supper.

Pairs often return to the same nest each year and add to it. These nests can reach up to eight feet long and hundreds of pounds. It is not uncommon for the nests to grow so heavy that the branches they sit on will break and the nests come crashing to the ground.

PONDER THIS

This eagle was named for an eighteenth-century zoologist and explorer, Georg Wilhelm Steller.

LEARN MORE·LEARN MORE·LEARN MORE·LEARN MORE·LEARN MORE·LEARN MORE·LEARN MORE·LEARN MORE·LEARN MORE·LEARN MORE

The San Diego Zoo and Natural Research Ltd. tracks the migration of sea eagles. To see the results visit: http://www.sandiegozoo.org/news/stellers_sea_eagle_tracking.html

ALL ABOUT THE STELLER'S SEA EAGLE

- Range: northeastern Russian coast, south to North Korea and Japan
- Habitat: tree-lined open river plains and rocky coastlines
- Diet: mostly fish, but also shellfish, crab, small animals, other birds, and carrion
- Length: 34 to 41 inches (86.5 to 105 cm); wingspan, up to 8 feet (2.5 m)
- Weight: females, 15 to 20 pounds (6.8 to 9 kg); males, 11 to 13 pounds (5 to 6 kg)

BUILD A NEST

Birds expend a lot of energy building nests so their young will have a safe place to grow. How would you survive as a bird parent? Try to build your own nest.

WHAT YOU NEED

- Large piece of sturdy cardboard placed on the counter or on a planting dish
- Nesting materials, such as sticks, twigs, yarn, grass, mud, or leaves
- 2 Ping-Pong balls

WHAT TO DO

1. Decide where you will build your nest. Use the flat cardboard or planting dish as the base.

2. Arrange the materials you have collected in the shape of a nest. Use mud or other material to hold the nest together. It might take a few tries until the nest is suitable.

3. Place the Ping-Pong balls into the nest. Do they stay put or roll out?

4. Think like a bird. If you were a bird in your neighborhood, where would you build your nest? Where would your eggs be safest from predators? What could you use in your nest that would help it stay hidden from predators?

SNOW MONKEY

The Japanese macaque lives throughout Japan, but it is known as the most northern-living non-human primate. These macaques live in the snow. When the weather is too chilly for them, however, they take a relaxing soak in natural hot springs. The Japanese macaque has brown or gray fur that grows thicker in the winter, a red face with no fur, and a very short tail. Macaques are ground-dwelling monkeys and live in groups called troops.

PONDER THIS

In the 1940s, researchers studied a troop of Japanese macaques. They lured them out of hiding by placing sweet potatoes on the sand. One female named Imo took her sand-covered sweet potato to the water and washed it off. She seemed to like the salty flavor the seawater added. She would dip her potato in the water, take a bite, then dip the potato again in the water.

One day, the researchers scattered grains of wheat on the sand. The other monkeys picked up the grains one by one, but Imo grabbed a handful of wheat and sand and threw it into the water. The sand sank but the wheat floated, making it easy to skim off the grains of wheat. The other monkeys in the troop learned from Imo and this behavior has been passed down through the generations.

ALL ABOUT THE JAPANESE MACAQUE

- Range: Japan
- Habitat: subtropical lowlands to sub-alpine forests
- Diet: fruit, plants, seeds, insects, bird eggs, and bark
- Body length: 31 to 37 inches (79 to 95 cm)
- Tail length: 4 inches (10 cm)
- Weight: males, 20 to 30 pounds (9 to 13.6 kg); females, 10 pounds (4.5 kg)

MONKEY TAG

WHAT YOU NEED

- Grassy playing area
- 3 people
- Beanbag

WHAT TO DO

1. Mark off the playing field with a start line ("forest") and a finish line ("water").

2. One person takes the beanbag. This is the "potato." The "monkey" with the potato must go from the forest to the water to "wash" the potato. The other 2 monkeys try to get the potato away by tagging the first monkey.

3. If the monkey with the potato gets tagged, the tagger gets the potato and a chance to try to wash it.

4. The monkey who makes it to the water without being tagged wins.

PLAY MONKEY IN THE MIDDLE

1. With the same 3 people, choose one person to be the monkey without the potato.

2. The other 2 monkeys pass the potato back and forth as they run from the forest to the water. If the monkey without the potato is able to snag the potato out of the air or tag either monkey while one is holding the potato, that monkey wins. If the two monkeys with the potato successfully make it to the water, they win.

3. Switch roles so everyone has a chance to be the "monkey in the middle."

LEARN MORE·LEARN MORE·LEARN MORE·LEARN MORE·LEARN MORE·LEARN MORE·

Watch Japanese macaques in real time at Jigokudani, a park in the mountains of central Honshu. Check out their website: www.jigokudani-yaenkoen.co.jp/english/top/english. Click on the Snow Monkey Livecam link.

Try It!

Take a handful of sesame seeds and sand or dirt and place into a large bucket of water. What happens?

INDEX